RUNNING A SCOUT GROUP

First Published — 1954

PRINTED BY
KENT PAPER COMPANY, LTD.,
ASHFORD, KENT.

RUNNING A SCOUT GROUP

by

J. F. COLQUHOUN, O.B.E.,
Headquarters Commissioner for Relationships,
Boy Scouts Association

THE BOY SCOUTS ASSOCIATION
25 Buckingham Palace Road
London, S.W.1

Three circles interlocking was an early Christian symbol for the Trinity in Unity. Geoffrey Fraser, the designer of the book jacket, has taken this symbol and extended it to represent the idea of the Unity there should be in the Group with its four interlocking sections of Cub, Scout, Senior Scout and Rover Scout. (Or it might be thought of as Cub, Scout, Rover Scout and Scouters.)

CONTENTS

EXPLANATIONS AND ABBREVIATIONS

A.C.M.	...	Assistant Cubmaster.
A.O.F.B.	...	Ancient Order of Frothblowers.
A.R.S.L.	...	Assistant Rover Scout Leader.
A.S.M.	...	Assistant Scoutmaster.
C.M.	...	Cubmaster.
D.C.	...	District Commissioner.
G.S.M.	...	Group Scoutmaster.
I.H.Q.	...	Imperial Headquarters of the Boy Scouts Association.
L.A.	...	Local Association.
L.E.A.	...	Local Education Authority.
P.L.	...	Patrol Leader.
P.O.R.	...	Policy, Organisation and Rules of the Boy Scouts Association.
R.S.L.	...	Rover Scout Leader.
S.M.	...	Scoutmaster.

SCOTLAND.—As Scotland has its own P.O.R., some passages in this book must be read in that country in conjunction with that P.O.R. For example, Scotland does not permit Senior Scout Troops; the "over-15s" are included in Troops with younger boys, but have separate activities on their own.

GROUP.—The complete unit of Wolf Cub Pack, Boy Scout Troop and Rover Scout Crew, with the addition, if desired, of a Senior Scout Troop. The term is used even if the unit lacks one or more of the sections.

SECTION.—One of the parts into which the Group is divided—*i.e.* Cub Pack, Boy Scout Troop, Senior Scout Troop, Rover Crew.

SCOUTER.—Any person who holds a warrant.

GROUP SCOUTER.—The term includes the G.S.M. and all the Scouters of the sections of the Group.

SCOUT in italics includes Wolf Cub, Boy Scout, Senior Scout and Rover Scout.

(S) in brackets after a title means Senior Scout.

FOREWORD

When, in 1908, the late Lord Baden-Powell answered the demand of the boys of Great Britain and founded the Boy Scout Movement, Scouts were grouped in Patrols, and when a couple or more Patrols were in being in a locality they became a Scout Troop. In 1916, the Wolf Cubs were started for the younger brothers of the Scouts and they were formed into Wolf Cub Packs. Two years later, yet another section was formed for the older Scouts—Rover Scouts.

Although there was quite frequently a loose connection between a Scout Troop, a Wolf Cub Pack and a Rover Patrol because they were connected with the same Church or used the same meeting-place or bore the same local number, each unit was practically independent. To-day the disadvantages of such an arrangement are obvious, but in the early 1920s we accepted it and, if a Cubmaster and Scoutmaster had just had a difference of opinion about the use of the meeting-place, the Cubs who were due to become Scouts were, no doubt, advised to join another Troop!

However, this all changed as a result of a revolutionary proposal made at the Open Conference at Bournemouth in 1927. The proposal was that the unit for organisational purposes should be the Scout Group with a Group Scoutmaster in charge of it, and the Conference received the suggestion with such enthusiasm that it became fact in January, 1928. And so was born the family of the Scout Group that we know to-day; the unit that a boy joins knowing he is expected to grow up in that family through the stages of Cub Pack, Scout Troop, Senior Troop and Rover Crew.

It is curious that I.H.Q. has never published itself, or had published, a handbook to help the Group Scoutmaster in his complex job. He is the guide, philosopher and friend to his team of Scouters, to the Group Committee, probably —and most desirably—to a branch of the B.-P. Guild of Old Scouts and, more than likely, to a Parents' or Supporters' Association. A Group of my acquaintance with strong training sections and Old Scouts, Group Committee and Supporters' Association, has about four hundred boys and adults connected with it; quite a task for the Group Scoutmaster! But now he has this most welcome book to help him. We are indeed fortunate that Mr. Colquhoun has been able to find the time in his busy life for Scouting to give G.S.M.s the benefit of his wide experience. He has set the seal to the proposal he made as long ago as 1927, for it was he who electrified that Bournemouth Conference with his suggestion of the Scout Group.

Scouting has much for which to thank Mr. Colquhoun, and I have little doubt that, in the years to come, " Running a Scout Group " will be regarded as one of the most valuable of his many valuable contributions to the Movement to which he and we are so proud to belong.

Chief Executive Commissioner.

June, 1954

AN EXCUSE FOR THIS BOOK

IT may be argued that there are too many books about Scouting already, and this argument receives some support when you look at the loaded shelves of books in The Scout Shop.

Why, then, inflict yet another book on an overstocked market? Isn't it all in "Scouting for Boys"?

Perhaps, then, I had better produce an excuse for writing this particular book. The fact is, it isn't all in "Scouting for Boys," and the Founder himself constantly threw out fresh tips as the Movement developed. Scouting has inevitably become more complicated since 1908. Wolf Cubs were tacked on at one end, Rover Scouts at the other; later came Senior Scouts. The old happy-go-lucky way of running things has long ceased to be good enough, and the Scout Group and the Group Scoutmaster are the result.

That is my excuse. There are all sorts of technical treatises on the tying of knots or the building of peculiar structures or the devising of special Pack evenings, but the man who has to supervise and co-ordinate the Group as a whole has no such book to help him with the job.

I hope that this book may be of some help to him, particularly if he is a newcomer, and even to the rest of the team which is associated with him. There is nothing very original in it—it is, indeed, no more than a compilation of material which I have found scattered about in many places, but that material is not easily available.

It is not an official publication, in the sense that every sentence has been approved by Imperial Headquarters. But much of it comes from official sources, such as "Policy, Organisation and Rules," Scouters' training course notes, and the like.

I must not end my excuse without expressing my indebtedness to Mr. E. G. Neate for his series of articles called "The Group comes of age" in "The Scouter" for 1949; for a similar series by various authors in 1946, and for the series called "Group Calendar" which appeared monthly in 1951 from the inventive minds of Messrs. Hurll and Hazlewood. They are well worth looking at, if you have access to the volumes of "The Scouter" for those years. I am indebted, too, to a host of Scouters, known and unknown, who have shared their experiences with me through the years. Last, and by no means least, I acknowledge an unrepayable debt to the 8th Holborn Group, through which I was brought into Scouting and with which I have been more or less loosely connected since 1918.

Both Mr. Hurll and Mr. Neate were kind enough to read the draft of this book, and I owe them my sincere thanks, not only for the labour involved, but also for many valuable suggestions.

CHAPTER 1

A SHORT HISTORY LESSON

BADEN-POWELL wrote " Scouting for Boys " in the hope that it might be found useful to existing organisations such as the Boys' Brigade, the Y.M.C.A., and the Churches. He had no idea of a Movement of his own.

But that great benefactor of Scouting, Sir Arthur Pearson, published " Scouting for Boys " in fortnightly parts in 1908, at a price which boys could afford to pay, or could persuade their mothers to give them. Thousands upon thousands of copies were sold, and Scout Patrols, formed by the boys themselves, sprang up all over the country. One can dimly imagine the chaos! B.-P. had to abandon his Army career, and get some sort of organisation going.

He was concerned at first for boys of eleven upwards, for whom " Scouting for Boys " was written. It was all quite simple, for it was only necessary to find a Scoutmaster, and the Troop was under way. The Scoutmaster had his Troop, and he was the boss.

But quite soon small boys clamoured at the Troop room door, or joined the bigger boys round the lamp-post, and in many cases the soft-hearted (and soft-headed) Scoutmaster let them join. By 1913 it was necessary to consider a junior section, and experiments were started with "Junior Scouts" or " Wolf Cubs." These experiments were so successful that B.-P. called a conference in 1916 and decided to add Wolf Cub sections to Boy Scout Troops, so that from 1917 there were Cubmasters (many of them ladies) in charge of Cub Packs and Scoutmasters in charge of Scout Troops.

Sometimes Pack and Troop were run quite independently of one another; more often the Scoutmaster was recognised as the Cubmaster's boss, even if he did not run the Cubs himself. But very soon B.-P. was being asked questions about the relationship of Cubmaster to Scoutmaster. " I have two and a half years' service," wrote one Cubmaster, " while the Scoutmaster has only eight months. He claims to hold absolute control over the Cubs and me." B.-P. had no strong views, it appears. He replied: "As regards the officers, I really don't know whether the Scoutmaster is more important than the Cubmaster, or vice versa, but in any case both are working with one common aim, and they will be considered on an equal standing as regards administration." I suspect that District Commissioners had to exercise a great deal of tact to soothe ruffled feelings. At the end of 1918, Headquarters had to give a ruling: " When a Pack is attached to a Troop, though the Scoutmaster will exercise general supervision, he will delegate the fullest amount of responsibility in the actual management of the Pack to the Cubmaster."

So far, so good. But, quite soon, Rover Scouts appeared on the scene and, being of a turbulent and independent frame of mind, were not content to accept their Scoutmaster's orders. They wanted leaders of their own, and not the men who had run them when they were small boys. No small uproar was heard in the land, and problems of co-ordination loomed larger and larger.

In November, 1926, the following notice appeared in " The Scouter ": "A proposal involving a great constitutional change has been made, and Imperial Headquarters invite general comment thereon.

(1) That Rover Leaders holding certain qualifications should be given warrants.

(2) That a Troop Council must be formed wherever three sections exist, and that one of its duties should be to elect the Chairman of the meeting, who would then be in control of the complete Troop.

It must be remembered that up to now the Scoutmaster has always been deemed to be the head of the complete Troop and has been warranted accordingly."

The whole subject was put down for discussion at the National Conference at Bournemouth in April, 1927. In the meantime, the welkin rang with the battle-cries of the contestants, especially those well-rooted Scoutmasters who felt that their vested interests were threatened. It all seems rather silly now, but it was great fun to watch at the time.

But when it came to the Bournemouth Conference, there was a completely unexpected consensus of opinion, and Headquarters got the lead they wanted. The two proposals quoted above found general favour—and that was the origin of what is now known as the Group system.

On 1st January, 1928, new rules came into force. Rover Leaders were given warrants. The combination of the three sections—Wolf Cub Pack, Boy Scout Troop and Rover Scout Crew—was thenceforth to be known as the Group. Most important of all, the rank of Group Scoutmaster was created, for the man who was to be in charge of the Group as a whole.

It was a grand thing for the Scout Movement that common sense prevailed amid all the clamour of conflicting views. But the Movement had not yet realised the importance of " the fourth man," as the G.S.M. was often called. The 1928 rules described the G.S.M. as a person who " might be the warranted Scouter in charge of one of the sections—or even a fourth person." As time went on, we came to recognise more and more clearly how important that " fourth man " was, and the rules were altered to give him due emphasis.

That is ancient history. But we have a long way to go yet before the full value of the Group system is universally recognised.

CHAPTER 2

THE SCOUT GROUP

"THE unit for *Scout* organisation in the District is the Group" (P.O.R. 168).

"The complete Group consists of Cub Pack, Scout Troop and Rover Scout Crew, with the addition, if desired, of a Senior Scout Troop; but may at any time consist of one or two sections only" (P.O.R. 176).

It must, therefore, be our aim to get our Groups complete, where this is not already the case, and to make them a real family unit, self-supporting and self-contained. Clearly, this will not be possible for such Groups as those in schools, universities and works, where limited age ranges are dealt with, and for some Groups in rural areas, which we shall discuss later in this chapter. But all others should make this their aim, and refuse to be satisfied until they are complete.

As Mr. Neate has remarked: "It was said long ago that every Scouter is a quite exceptional man or woman, dealing with a quite unusual collection of boys in unparalleled circumstances bristling with unique difficulties." All too often, Scouters who offer excuses of this kind are just individualists, who "don't hold with Cubs," or can't keep their senior boys. It is one of the District Commissioner's more delicate jobs to try to convert such people to the proper use of the Group system, by showing them the vital necessity for it in the interest of the boys themselves who, after all, are the people for whom Scouting is provided.

The importance of the Group as a family unit is that—

(i) it provides continuous training from a boy's entry as a Cub at the age of eight, up to the Rover section;

(ii) it ensures that such training is progressive, that the boy's widening interests are catered for, and that each boy is continually increasing his knowledge, and particularly his realisation of the full meaning of the *Scout* Law and Promise;

(iii) it avoids overlapping between the various sections;

(iv) it helps the boy to proceed happily from one section to another when the time comes, as he proceeds from class to class in the same school;

(v) it makes all the Scouters friendly colleagues, instead of strangers or even rivals;

(vi) it brings in the help of lay men and women to relieve the Scouters of a great deal of work and leave them free to attend to the individual training of each boy.

The size of the Group

No hard and fast rule can be laid down for the size of the Group; so much depends upon the boy-population available and the help which can be obtained. But it may be said that the boys themselves like to belong to a fairly large show, that greater competition and more varied activities become possible and, of course, that Scouting becomes available to a greater number. But as mass training is completely opposed to the Founder's teaching, and the Scouter's knowledge of each boy must be as complete as possible, we must be careful not to overstep the line.

The great majority of Scout Groups are found in well-populated areas, and Groups of 100-120 should be our general aim, but for many years past the average size of a Group in this country has been about 40. This is surely much too low, for a Group of 40 usually consists of no more than 20 Cubs, 15 Boy Scouts and 5 over 15 years of age. A Group of 100 might consist of 30 Cubs, 36 Boy Scouts, 24 Senior Scouts and 10 Rovers, and there are many Groups which find this possible. We should make something like this our aim wherever the boy population can provide the recruitment. If a proper staff of Scouters can be enrolled, the individual training of the boys can be amply safeguarded. It has been found possible in many hundreds of well-established Groups, and it seems to be a fact that it is easier to recruit Scouters for a big and flourishing Group.

Some Groups in thickly-populated areas have found their waiting-lists of boys growing so long that they have started a second Pack or a second Troop within the same Group. There is nothing against this in our rules, and indeed it has much to recommend it, if suitable accommodation for meetings is available.

Formation of a Group

" No steps may be taken for the formation of a new Group without the provisional sanction of the local Association and the District Commissioner " (P.O.R. 177).

But how often is that wise rule ignored, either through ignorance or over-enthusiasm? It is not at all unusual for the Commissioner to discover, often by pure chance, that a Group, or more often a section of a Group, has been started without his sanction, frequently on wrong lines. Someone asks him: " Do you know that there is a Troop at ——?" He hastens round at the first opportunity and finds a disorderly rabble of youngsters and a bewildered adult trying to cope with them, without plan or equipment. He has to unravel the tangle and make up his mind whether the man in charge is suitable for a warrant, and everything is so much more difficult than it need have been if the rule had been complied with.

It is difficult to know how to avoid such wrong starts, for the promoter is probably ignorant of 177 or any other rule in P.O.R., but if any Scouter in the District hears that a new Group is being launched in this way, he will be a great help to the District Commissioner if he passes the information to him at once.

It must be obvious that careful planning and consultation are essential before any announcement is made to the boys of the neighbourhood that a Group or section is to be started. What kind of Group is it to be? Is it to be sponsored or open? Is there room for another Group in the neighbourhood? Who are to be the Scouters? Are they suitable and are there enough of them? If they are quite inexperienced, what help can be offered to them by the District until they have gained some experience? What money will be available? Is lay support being enlisted right at the start? Is a beginning to be made with a Pack or Troop, or can both start at the same time? What accommodation can be obtained?

Ideally, I believe that the first Scouter to be obtained is the Group Scoutmaster, for he is the planner and should be on the scene at the beginning. It is he who should discuss the plans with the District Commissioner, get the accommodation, gather a team of prospective Scouters and lay people round him, before the local boys know anything about it.

Imperial Headquarters publish two useful pamphlets, " How to start a Pack " and " How to start a Troop "—the result of much experience—and it is well to study these when the local plans are being made. I do not propose to go into details here, except to stress the injunction " Start small." Take in a few boys to start with, so that by the time you are ready to open the doors to all and sundry, you will have some Patrol Leaders or Sixers to give the others a lead.

Copies of the pamphlet, " The Group Committee," should also be available for lay supporters.

Sponsored or Open?

A Group is known as " sponsored " if it is connected with one of the bodies listed in P.O.R. 179. Most sponsored

Groups are connected with a Church, a school or an institution such as a hospital, but the rule should be consulted if the full list is needed. Groups not so "sponsored" are "open."

Sponsored Groups are fully dealt with in Chapter 11. It is clearly necessary to decide at the outset whether a new Group is to be sponsored or open. If it is to be sponsored, the Sponsoring Authority (*i.e.* "the person or committee appointed by the body concerned to exercise the functions with respect to such a Group," as P.O.R. expresses it) must be consulted as to all the plans, must sign the application for registration, and nominate all the Scouters.

About half the Groups in this country are sponsored by a Church or some other body; the other half are open. It is for the District Commissioner and Local Association to decide in which category a new Group shall fall, after full consultation with all concerned, and Headquarters will not interfere with their discretion. But where there are so few boys in a place that there would not be room for more than one Group, it is strongly recommended that the Group should be an open one, so that no boy shall be debarred from Scouting by reason of his religion or his school.

Registration of a Group

"All Groups must be registered at I.H.Q. and are recognised by the Boy Scouts Association only whilst so registered. Members of unregistered Groups who wear badges or in any way represent themselves as members of the Association are liable to prosecution as in Rule 23" (P.O.R. 178).

The procedure for the registration of a Group is laid down in P.O.R. There are special provisions for sponsored Groups, which will be dealt with in Chapter 11. As regards all Groups, the prospective Scouter in charge (who will, let us hope, have already consulted the local Scout authorities as to its formation) applies for registration on form C in triplicate to either the District Commissioner or the Local Association. It is their joint duty to satisfy themselves that " registration is desirable, that the Group will be properly conducted, that suitable Scouters are forthcoming, and that the prospective Scouter in charge accepts the aims, methods and policy of the Association, and undertakes to use his best endeavours to—

(1) form a Group Committee as soon as possible, and in any case not later than three months after the date of registration;

(2) develop in due course a complete Group, unless conditions make this impossible;

(3) give due emphasis to the religious aspect of Scouting, and the claims of religion in the conduct and life of the Group;

(4) ensure that the various sections of the Group receive the full *Scout* training in character, health, handicraft and service;

(5) help the Group to obtain suitable headquarters and the necessary equipment and opportunities for training;

(6) comply in the case of a sponsored Group of any kind with any particular provisions of P.O.R. relating to such a Group (P.O.R. 182).

When they are satisfied on all these points, the D.C. and L.A. sign the three forms C and send them to I.H.Q., who issue a " Notification of Registration " to the prospective Scouter in charge, through the Secretary of the Local Association.

The Group is then formally registered and its members are entitled to regard themselves as members of the Boy Scouts Association.

Registration of Sections of Groups

As we have already seen, the Group is the unit which is registered, and it is registered as a Group even if at the beginning it consists only of a Cub Pack or a Scout Troop. If at a later stage it is desired to add another section to an existing Group, the written approval of the L.A. and D.C. is required, but no further registration is necessary at I.H.Q. (P.O.R. 194). I.H.Q. will know when they receive the annual census returns which are made by each Group.

Changes in Registration, and Transfers

It sometimes happens that a Group wishes to change its registered title, or to alter the nature of its registration (*i.e.* from " open " to " sponsored " or vice versa), or to be transferred from one Local Association to a neighbouring one, but it cannot do any of these things on its own. It must apply to the L.A. and D.C. for permission, but form C.2 is then used instead of form C, but still in triplicate (P.O.R. 187).

Renewal of Registration

A new Group is registered only up to 31st March, but renewal is a very simple matter. I.H.Q. ask for an annual re-registration, accompanied by certain statistics (known as the " census ") and a list of the Scouters of the Group, at 31st March each year. If that simple form is completed punctually by the G.S.M. and sent through the L.A. Secretary to I.H.Q., the Group is automatically re-registered. If it is not, the Group ceases to be registered, with unpleasant results if it thereafter carries on as a Group. Legally, its members are liable to prosecution if they continue to wear badges or to represent themselves as " Boy Scouts." In practice, they find life difficult because they can no longer buy badges for their boys, who get very cross if they do not quickly get the proficiency badges they have earned.

If a Group does find itself de-registered as the result of

neglect to send in this form, it can apply for re-registration, but it has to go through the formalities of filling up form C (in triplicate), and so on.

Sea Scouts and Air Scouts

There are branches of Scouting known as Sea Scouts and Air Scouts, which are designed to attract boys whose special interest is on the water or in the air, and who might not otherwise be brought into Scouting. In forming a new Group, it should be considered whether it should include either of these branches. It all depends upon whether real facilities and an expert staff are available.

Sea Scouting need not, of course, be carried out on the sea. Indeed, it may be easier to run a good Sea Scout Group on inland waters such as rivers, canals, lakes and reservoirs, for many of our coastal waters are dangerous for small boats. But there must be activities on the water; and these seem to have a special appeal for senior boys. For this reason, some Groups prefer their Boy Scout section to be an ordinary Troop, while their Senior Scouts form a Sea Scout Patrol or Troop.

Air Scouting must be genuine. Even if facilities for flying are not available, there should be opportunities for visits to aerodromes and for inspecting aircraft. It follows that the Air Scout branch is a comparatively small one.

Books and pamphlets on these special subjects are obtainable from I.H.Q., but the following points should be borne in mind by G.S.M.s: —

(i) Sea Scouting and Air Scouting are first and foremost Scouting, and all the main principles and activities of Scouting apply. The sea and air elements are additional, and subsidiary. Eccentricities of uniform should not be permitted.

(ii) It is not necessary for the G.S.M. to be an expert on the water or in the air, provided that he recruits experts to help him.

(iii) The training of Wolf Cubs remains the same in any kind of Group. There are no such animals as Sea Cubs or Air Cubs.

(iv) Safety precautions must be rigidly observed. (These are discussed on pages 165-167.)

(v) Recognition can be obtained from the Admiralty and Air Ministry for a limited number of Sea and Air Scout Troops which reach specified standards. Particulars can be obtained from I.H.Q.

(vi) In the case of Sea Scouts, special Committees are set up by Counties to see that safety precautions are carried out and that help and advice are available to Groups.

(vii) Special permission is required from the County Commissioner before an ordinary Scout Group may change to being an Air Scout Group.

Handicapped Scouts

One of the great triumphs of Scouting is that it can be adapted to boys who are physically or mentally handicapped, and there is much expert testimony to the value of Scouting in maintaining and improving the morale of such boys.

A word will be said, in the chapter on sponsored Groups, about Scout Groups in hospitals and institutions (page 126). But there are many handicapped boys who live at home, and some of them can become members of ordinary Groups. It does such a lot of good to the boy himself, and the other boys will take pride in looking after him. Even a bedridden boy can become a *Scout,* if visits to his home can be arranged by Scouters, Patrol Leaders, or other *Scouts* who live near to him. It is, however, a mistake to introduce too many handicapped boys into an ordinary Group; one per Patrol is probably the limit.

In all cases, the boy's Scouting should be as normal as possible. He can wear uniform and progress through the ordinary lines of *Scout* training. Special tests are available in place of the activities which he cannot undertake, and can be found in an I.H.Q. pamphlet, "Alternative Tests for Handicapped Scouts." The permission of the District Commissioner must be obtained before a *Scout* in a normal Group can take such tests.

School Groups

Groups sponsored by schools will be dealt with in Chapter 11. It must be admitted that in some cases promising boys have been taken away from ordinary Groups to become members of school Groups in the neighbourhood. Such a step is bound to cause hard feelings, and should be avoided by school Scouters. There are usually plenty of boys in the school who are not *Scouts* already. But G.S.M.s of ordinary Groups must use common sense in dealing with this problem, and must remember that some of their boys might not be able to fit Scouting in with their school commitments unless they did their Scouting at school.

It is very desirable that *Scouts* at boarding schools should join their local Group during the holidays. Normally, under P.O.R. 198, a *Scout* cannot be a member of more than one Group, but this rule is relaxed in the case of a boy at boarding school. He can also be a member of his local Group, which can be a great help to him in continuing his training and passing his tests during the holidays.

Pamphlets on the formation of Scout Groups in schools are obtainable from I.H.Q., entitled " Scouting in Preparatory Schools " and " Scouting in Secondary Schools."

Rural areas

Scouting in rural areas has special problems of its own. While the emphasis on outdoor activities is easy, boys are few, distances are great, and there is a constant shortage of suitable Scouters. Nevertheless, Scouting can be run successfully for small numbers, and in that we have an advantage over most of the other boys' organisations. We should not let the difficulties prevent us from trying to increase the number of Scout Groups in the villages.

It may well be that the shortage of manpower will not allow for a separate G.S.M. without other duties, but even in villages it should be our aim to find one. Until we have found one, a local layman, who will be Chairman of the Group Committee and give opportunities for the Scouters (if there are more than one) to meet together, will do very well as a substitute. Help is often obtainable from such organisations as the British Legion, the Young Farmers' Clubs and the Women's Institutes, if the need is made known.

In villages which have no Scout Group, it is worth trying to find someone who would be known as "A Friend of Scouting" and who would be linked with the Scout Movement by becoming a member of the Local Association. His (or her) duties would be to help boys to join a Troop in a neighbouring village, if possible, and to watch for any opportunities of getting a Troop or Pack started in the village if a prospective Scouter comes over the horizon.

It is sometimes possible to form a neighbourhood Troop with a Patrol in each of a number of villages. This lends emphasis to the Patrol system, as B.-P. intended. Each Patrol conducts its weekly programme in its own village, while all the Patrols come together, say once a month, for the Troop meeting, and the Patrols visit each other from time to time. It is no use to say that such a scheme cannot be worked, for it is the ordinary pattern of Scouting in some countries, but it depends a good deal upon finding at least one good Scouter who will be able to train the Patrol Leaders and who has a car or a bicycle with which he can visit the village Patrols from time to time.

No one need be deterred because there are not enough boys of suitable ages to have both a Cub Pack and a Scout Troop. A Group may consist of only one section, and there are plenty of cases on record where a Cub Pack became a Scout Troop as the boys reached Scout age, and the Pack had to close because the village did not happen to possess enough boys of Cub age at that time.

As so many boys are now transported to school by bus, a Troop may be registered at a central school and have its meetings there before the boys disperse to their villages. In such a case, it is useful to compose the Patrols of boys from the same village, so that the Patrol can continue its Scouting when it gets home and at week-ends.

The good Group

It is one thing to form a Group: it is quite another to make it a good Group, a recognised part of the local community, to which boys and adults alike are proud to belong. Too many of our Groups are hidden away in a corner, as if they were ashamed of Scouting. That is a poor preparation for growing boys. It is our job to prepare them to be good citizens in a community, not apart from it.

So we want the community to be interested in the Group and to like the way the *Scouts* behave in public, at school or work, and at home. The good Group is a kind of power house of energy and service to those around it, and that can only be done if the community is wired up to it.

It is not one man's job, although there may well be one long-established and attractive personality round whom the whole Group revolves. Lucky indeed is the Group that has such a G.S.M., but even he cannot do much without a good team to work with him. The team-work is even more important, and can produce an excellent Group without any outstanding personality. But someone must be at the head, and we shall consider in the next chapter what manner of man he is.

CHAPTER 3

THE GROUP SCOUTMASTER

WE have already seen in Chapter 1 how the idea of a "fourth man," in charge of the whole Group, grew as the Movement developed.

P.O.R. 169 now makes the definite statement that "it is important that a G.S.M. should be appointed even though the Group may at the time consist of one section only," except where it can never comprise more than one section, as in some schools and institutions. It goes on to say that "it is most desirable that the G.S.M. should be a person not holding any other warrant, or performing any other functions, in the Group."

Where a Scouter already holding a warrant in the Group seems the best person to be appointed G.S.M., every effort is to be made to relieve him of his existing duties by appointing someone else.

The duty of selection falls upon the D.C. and L.A., but they must consult the Group Council where the Group consists of more than one section. In the case of a sponsored Group, the Sponsoring Authority has his rights, but that will be discussed in Chapter 11.

Where no separate G.S.M. can be found for the time being, one of the Scouters in charge of a section must carry out the duties. Where the Group consists of only one section, the Scouter in charge of that section acts; where there are two or more sections, the D.C. and L.A., after consulting the Group Council, will choose whichever Scouter seems best qualified by character, age and experience.

In other words, someone must be in charge of the whole Group, and it must wherever possible be a man without other duties.

Certainly, the G.S.M. will usually be a man, but P.O.R. does add that a warrant as G.S.M. may be issued to a lady under exceptional circumstances, but I.H.Q. will require a special recommendation by the L.A. or D.C., with a full statement of the exceptional circumstances and an assurance that the Senior Scouts and Rovers in the Group will be in charge of a man (P.O.R. 170). Not only the circumstances, but the lady must be exceptional.

Where a G.S.M. is confronted with a vacancy in the leadership of a section, he may take charge of the section with the approval of the D.C. and L.A., but this must be regarded as a purely temporary measure, and an additional warrant for the rank concerned will not be applied for (P.O.R. 174). Moreover, a G.S.M. must not personally take charge of a Rover Crew unless he possesses the special qualifications required for that rank.

Although the Group system has been in existence since 1928, we are still very short of G.S.M.s in the full sense of that expression, and I would strongly urge that greater efforts should be made to obtain them. Shortage of manpower is pleaded as an excuse, but too often it is not realised that a separate G.S.M. is able to get more Scouters for the Group, if he is the right man. When we come to consider the duties which fall to a G.S.M., we must be convinced that it is quite impossible for a Scouter who is looking after a section to cover all of them. Most of them go by default; those which are accomplished can only be carried out at the expense of the boys for whose training he is responsible or by devoting a disproportionate amount of time, at the expense of his home duties and other interests.

Here let me quote a paragraph from a valuable report on "The Use and Recruitment of Manpower," issued by I.H.Q. in 1950. (Every G.S.M. should have a copy of it and check his manpower problems by reference to it.) The report says: "We would like to say with all the force of which we are capable that no difficulties of manpower must ever be solved by putting Scouting first and the claims of a Scouter's wife or family or career second. Between Scouting and family life there must be no conflict of loyalties, and we ask the co-operation of all Commissioners and Scouters in seeing that married Scouters are not allowed, let alone encouraged, to give such time to their Scouting interests that their family and married life suffer."

The special qualifications of a G.S.M.

P.O.R. 172 lays down the special qualifications of a G.S.M. as follows: —

(1) A general knowledge of "Scouting for Boys," "The Wolf Cub's Handbook," "Rovering to Success," P.O.R., and current Senior Scout literature.

(Although a G.S.M. need not be technically proficient in the work of any section, he must at least know what their methods are, as set out in the official handbooks, and particularly in the books written by the Founder himself.)

(2) Ability to obtain the use of suitable accommodation for *Scout* meetings.

(This is discussed later, in Chapter 8.)

(3) Age sufficient to enable him to carry out the work satisfactorily. The D.C. and L.A. will consider the suitability of the applicant for a G.S.M.'s warrant in this respect, particularly in relation to the ages of the other Scouters in the Group. Normally, a warrant will not be issued as G.S.M. to anyone under the age of 30, but in an exceptional case, with the special sanction of the County Commissioner, a reduction of the minimum age to 25 may be permitted.

The G.S.M.'s duties

John Thurman, the Camp Chief, has written that the duties of the G.S.M. can be summed up as follows: ". . . to co-ordinate the work of the sections of the Group, to relieve the Scouters who are running sections of as much administration work as possible and to act as principal liaison officer between Scouting and parents, and Scouting and the public. Enough for anyone to undertake in his spare time."

P.O.R. 173 defines his functions in six paragraphs: —

(1) To develop in due course a complete Group, as defined in Rule 170, unless conditions make this impossible.

(2) To exercise general supervision over all sections of the Group and to co-ordinate their activities, whilst delegating the fullest amount of responsibility in their actual management to the Scouters in charge of them.

(3) To act as Chairman of the Group Council under Rule 201 (ii), and to encourage co-operation between the Scouters of the Group.

(4) To secure the formation of a Group Committee under Rule 202, and to serve on it himself.

(5) To deal with matters relating to the membership of *Scouts* in accordance with Rules 197-199.

(6) To ensure that contact is maintained with members of the Group serving in the Forces.

It should be added that for all this he is responsible to the L.A. and D.C., and also, in the case of a sponsored Group, to the Sponsoring Authority.

When we were discussing the formation of a new Group in Chapter 2, we found that under P.O.R. 182 the prospective Scouter in charge was required to undertake to use his best endeavours to secure a number of things, some of which also appear above in the list of the G.S.M.'s functions. But we must remember four other points from P.O.R. 182: —

(i) to give due emphasis to the religious aspect of Scouting, and the claims of religion in the conduct and life of the Group;

(ii) to ensure that the various sections of the Group receive the full *Scout* training in character, health, handicraft and service;

(iii) to help the Group to obtain suitable headquarters and the necessary equipment and opportunities for training;

(iv) to comply in the case of a sponsored Group of any kind with any particular provisions of P.O.R. relating to such a Group.

These and many other matters will be dealt with in greater detail as the book proceeds.

It need only be added here that it is an implicit obligation on all G.S.M.s, and especially the new ones, to make themselves as efficient as possible. Training courses for G.S.M.s, lasting over a week-end, are provided at Gilwell Park and other training centres and are advertised in " The Scouter." The G.S.M. who can manage to spare time will also be amply rewarded by attending the preliminary training courses for Cub and Scout leaders which are held all over the country, and later taking a Wood Badge course, which is described under the heading of " Training " in Chapter 4.

He will also need to be up to date in his reading, keeping touch with new developments and changes of rules published in " The Scouter," and seeing that his Scouters are aware of them.

Uniform for G.S.M.s

" G.S.M.s wear uniform as in Rule 291," says P.O.R., and the new G.S.M. will find he has a choice of garments, both upper and nether. Whatever he chooses, he will wish to set the example to the members of the Group in neatness, suitability and adherence to the rules. As B.-P. himself said, " You are the model to your boys and your smartness will reflect itself in them." And the Manpower Report stated: " It is only necessary to visit any rally to see monstrosities in uniform, which may be satisfying to the wearer, but are thoroughly bad publicity for the Movement and are a definite deterrent to recruiting members of the public."

"Alternatives are available for Scouters' uniform, and each Scouter will be wise to study his own figure and appearance. Short sleeves and shorts do not suit everybody, and no one can do good work while feeling slightly ridiculous—or looking ridiculous to his wife and friends! "

" Hence, we draw attention to the recent declaration that trousers ought not to be regarded as an oddity as a part of the uniform of the Scouter, and that Commissioners and Group Scoutmasters of the older generation might well set the example by wearing them."

What kind of a man is the G.S.M.?

The G.S.M. sets the example, in his daily life, of practising fully the Scout Promise and Law. No man can lead others along the Scout road unless he himself believes in, and practises, the principles of Scouting. He should, therefore, publicly take the Scout Promise when receiving his warrant.

As a G.S.M., he is a leader of men and women rather than of boys, and must know how to handle people—often rather sensitive and prickly people—with tact and good humour. Tact may be required in large quantities in the course of his supervision of the other Scouters and in dealing with the occasional irate parent.

But being tactful does not mean being weak. When things need to be put right, firmness and persistence will be required, but they can be exercised with gentleness and patience and without any appearance of dictatorship.

The G.S.M. should be sufficiently mature (and that is why an age of not less than 30 is ordinarily expected) to have a good knowledge of the world. His judgment will then be respected by Scouters, parents and committee members, and this will be of immense value if some serious trouble should unfortunately arise.

He must be a " planner," if you like the modern jargon, not only making arrangements for the present but taking also a long-term view of the Group and its needs.

He must be the kind of man who can ask and obtain help from outsiders and parents, and deal amicably and on equal terms with clergy, schoolmasters and local officials.

In all this, he must keep a constant watch on himself to see that he does not try to do all the work himself, but that he spreads it out as widely as possible, leaving the maximum of responsibility to the other Scouters and officials of the Group.

A sense of humour does not come amiss.

Where to find G.S.M.s

There is much about this in the Manpower Report, and I again commend a study of it. Here is one brief quotation: "The only valid test in Scouting is fitness for the job. It does not follow that a successful Scouter of a section, who knows how to lead boys, will make a good Commissioner or Group Scoutmaster, for their job is to lead men. No one should feel aggrieved that he has not been given a particular job, or say that 'he has not been promoted.' In this sense, there is no promotion in Scouting."

It may well be wise to look outside the Movement for your G.S.M.—among the Old Scouts, or parents, or lay members, or those as yet quite unconnected with Scouting. On the other hand, it may be time for your Scoutmaster to have a change of job, if he no longer relishes the joys of camping or of a strenuous hike as much as he used to do.

It may perhaps appear that all the qualities required of a G.S.M., as indicated in the foregoing pages, cannot be expected of any one man. I utterly refuse to believe it. There are thousands upon thousands of men in this country who are fully armed with the necessary attributes, if only we can persuade them that Scouting is worth while, and that they are sharing the duties with a loyal and enthusiastic team. This is not just theory. There are thousands of them already doing the job, but many more are needed.

CHAPTER 4

THE SCOUTERS AND THEIR WARRANTS

THE G.S.M. may well feel that the most important people in the Group are the Scouters in charge of the sections, and their assistants, for it is they who exert direct influence upon the boys. When things are going well, he is in the background. But it is his job to make them into a happy, friendly and harmonious team, each one enthusiastic about the work he is doing, while not underrating the efforts of the Scouters in other sections.

It is also the G.S.M.'s responsibility to see that the Group is adequately staffed and that vacancies are filled without delay.

The minimum staff of Scouters

We have always been short of Scouters. Although the census figures show that some Groups have plenty of them, most Groups have too few. The *minimum* requirements for a Group of four sections should be—

1 Group Scoutmaster without other duties.
2 Pack Scouters.
2 Scouters for the Boy Scout Troop.
2 Scouters for the Senior Scout Troop.
1 Scouter for the Rover Crew.
—
8
—

At any rate that gives us a target to aim at, but we should not be satisfied with that. A full Pack or Troop can absorb the energies of three or even more Scouters. If we reach that number, no Scouter need be called upon to give up too much of his leisure.

As the Camp Chief has said, "We want more people doing less, better."

We shall consider the particular requirements of each section later on in this chapter.

The recruitment of Scouters

Our aim in recruiting Scouters can be expressed in the slogan, " The right man in the right job at the right time."

We must, unfortunately, face the fact that a G.S.M. may sometimes find it difficult to recruit new Scouters until he has got rid of an unsuitable man or woman who holds a warrant in the Group now. Some people prove to have no talent for handling boys; others grow old and stale; others get slack; still others are too occupied in their business or at home. The G.S.M. must be quite firm with such people, for it is the boys who count and not the adults. Sometimes the difficulty can be solved by offering the Scouter a more suitable form of service in the Group or in the Movement. The L.A. and D.C. may well be asked to confer honorary rank on a retiring Scouter who has given good service in the past (P.O.R. 165-166).

As regards the recruitment of new leaders, we must look to our own ranks first. We have always reared a great number of young leaders from our Rovers and older Scouts and we can feel proud that a recent statistical survey showed that 80 per cent of our Scouters had been brought up in the Movement. But we know that this problem of recruitment would be solved if we succeeded in keeping a larger proportion of our boys up to the stage of young manhood. It is one of the most important jobs of the G.S.M. and the Group Council to give constant attention to this point, and especially to bridge the awkward gap of National Service (see pages 151-153).

While the G.S.M. bears the final responsibility for obtaining new leaders, he will have many helpers in his task—the other Scouters, members of the Group Committee, parents, friends and supporters of the Group, all should keep their eyes open in their own circle of friends and relations.

What about the boys themselves? In the early days of Scouting, many small gangs of boys found their own Scoutmasters among the general public. Why not now? They have a shrewd idea as to the type of man they would like as a Scouter, and should be encouraged to look for him. If a boy has a suggestion, let him put it to the Court of Honour through his Patrol Leader, and then let the G.S.M., after making the usual enquiries of I.H.Q., authorise the P.L. to approach the unsuspecting victim. It is much more difficult to refuse a deputation of keen youngsters standing on the doorstep and not knowing when to go away, than to say " No " to an adult.

I am sure that we lose many suitable men and women because we try to catch them too quickly. They are apt to regard Scouters as a collection of cranks and fanatics, expert in many of the higher mysteries of knots and first-aid and signalling and all the rest. So play your fish before you try to land him. Here again, let the boys in the Troop or Pack help you. Ask your victim to come down one evening and see the boys, or to visit a week-end camp. The sight of the boys' happiness and enthusiasm, and his conversation with them, may well be more effective than all your grown-up pleading.

Instructors

That leads me to the question of Instructors, which were used much more in the early days of the Movement than they are now. There are many thousands of men and women (many of them parents of *Scouts*) who are experts on some subject contained in the *Scout* tests, and who would be prepared to give a limited amount of time to teaching it to a small gang of boys. They can most effectively supplement the work of the Scouters, who are then left more free to perform their proper task, namely, to get to know each boy really well and to give him the special attention and the feeling of security which he needs.

But beware of the fanatic, who refuses to believe that he can deal with his pet subject in anything less than two hours at a time!

In addition to Instructors from outside, help of this kind can be obtained for Boy Scout Troops and Cub Packs from Rovers and Senior Scouts.

The Cubs have still further sources of supply, for some members of the Boy Scout Troop may be available. The Scoutmaster may well be glad to give an opportunity to a boy who has gained his First Class Badge (P.O.R. 225). Moreover, the Movement has for many years been fortunate in getting the services of a number of Rangers and Cadets from Girl Guide Companies. It is only tactful to ask the Guider for permission first! Still further help is sometimes forthcoming from girls who are not Girl Guides, and such help is very welcome if the girls are over 16 and keen on the job.

These useful folk can be called " Cub Instructors " and wear a special badge (P.O.R. 225).

The Scouters of the Pack

The special qualifications required for Cubmasters and Assistant Cubmasters are: —

(1) A general knowledge of " Scouting for Boys," " The Wolf Cub's Handbook," and P.O.R.

(2) Age for C.M., not less than 20; for A.C.M., not less than 18 (P.O.R. 214).

These are, of course, in addition to the general qualifications which apply to all Scouters, and which will be set out when we come to " Warrants " later in the chapter.

It should be noted, in connection with our consideration of the minimum number of Scouters above, that P.O.R. 216 says that " to ensure continuity, it is most desirable that every Pack should have one A.C.M., and, where a Pack consists of more than three Sixes, additional A.C.M.s are desirable."

Ladies are, in general, more suitable as Cubmasters, and the Movement owes much to their enthusiasm and devoted service down the years. But there is a type of man who is specially gifted in dealing with boys of Cub age (and can usually manage no other age range), and if you find one of them, he is worth his weight in gold. But whether you have a man or a woman as Cubmaster, it is very desirable to have help from the other sex, and one man, whether as C.M. or A.C.M., should be attached to every Pack. He is usually better able to deal with the physical side of Cubbing, although I have seen on a Wood Badge course wide game a girl bring down a young Rugger player with as fine a tackle round the knees as you could see at Twickenham. Moreover, there comes a time round about the age of 10 when a Cub instinctively turns to a man rather than a woman, and a male A.C.M. can often hold on to a youngster at that age until he is old enough to go into the Troop.

A number of our Pack Scouters are recruited from the local Girl Guides, and we are very grateful to our sisters for the help they give us. "A Guide or Ranger helping with a Pack may be given permission by the Captain of the Guide Company to wear Guide uniform, when so helping," together with the appropriate Cub badge (P.O.R. 299). Where a Guider is also a Scouter, she " may wear her blue coat and skirt or overall with the appropriate hat, badge, and scarf or green tie for all *Scout* functions " (P.O.R. 301).

The Scouters of the Boy Scout Troop

The special qualifications for Scoutmaster and Assistant Scoutmaster are: —

(1) A general knowledge of " Scouting for Boys," " The Wolf Cub's Handbook," " Rovering to Success," P.O.R., and current Senior Scout literature.

(2) Age for S.M., not less than 20; for A.S.M., not less than 18 (P.O.R. 233).

An A.S.M. is most desirable, and where a Troop consists of more than four Patrols, additional A.S.M.s are desirable (P.O.R. 235).

Groups have the choice, under the rules, as to whether they run a separate Senior Scout Patrol or Troop, or leave the Scouts who are over 15 in the Boy Scout Troop, ensuring that for part of their time they are given activities suitable to their age. This is mentioned here only because it affects the staffing of the Boy Scout Troop, for if it contains Scouts of over 15, an additional Scouter who can deal properly with that age range is very necessary.

Scouters of this section must be of an age to do active things with their boys, and should give way to younger men when they are getting too old to enjoy doing them any longer.

Because the Patrol system is vital to Scouting, the Scoutmaster and his Assistants must use it. This will come up again later, but is mentioned here because the G.S.M., in selecting men for this section, must make it quite clear that it is their job to train the Patrol Leaders and give full authority to the Court of Honour. It is no use putting in a man who insists upon doing everything himself.

A warrant as S.M. or A.S.M. will only be issued to a lady at the discretion of I.H.Q. in exceptional circumstances, after considering a special recommendation submitted by the L.A. and D.C. (P.O.R. 232). Such recommendations usually come from the rural areas and there is no doubt that some ladies, with very special qualities, have done excellent work in leading Scout Troops in such areas. The Movement is also grateful to the many women who stepped into the breach during the two wars, but they are the first to give way to a man when one becomes available.

The Scouters of the Senior Scout Troop

Groups which run a Senior Scout Patrol or Troop for their boys who are over 15 will need Scouters to run them, and those Scouters should not also be Scouters in the Boy Scout Troop. A boy of 15 needs a change of Scouter, and the man who knows just how to handle boys of 14 and below is frequently a complete failure with those above that age.

The special qualifications for Scoutmaster and Assistant Scoutmaster of a Senior Scout Troop (known as S.M.(S) and A.S.M.(S)) are: —

(1) A general knowledge of "Scouting for Boys," "The Wolf Cub's Handbook," "Rovering to Success," P.O.R., and current Senior Scout literature.

(2) Age for S.M.(S), not less than 25. Age for A.S.M.(S), not less than 21.

(3) No person holding any other warrant in the same Troop, except that of G.S.M., may be appointed to either of these ranks (P.O.R. 247C).

Similar provision is made as regards A.S.M.s(S) as for A.S.M.s in the Boy Scout Troop.

Under no circumstances will a warrant for either rank be granted to a lady (P.O.R. 247B).

Particular care needs to be taken in choosing the Scouters for this section. Many of the boys are at work, and all are facing the acute problem of growing up. They require a handling which is both firm and sympathetic. Above all, they need someone whom they trust so fully that they will take their problems to him. The ideal combination is an older man as S.M.(S) with experience of life, and an A.S.M.(S) of youth and vigour who will share their hikes and expeditions with them.

The Scouters of the Rover Crew

The special qualifications for Rover Scout Leader and Assistant Rover Scout Leader are: —

(1) A general knowledge of "Scouting for Boys," "Rovering to Success," P.O.R., and current Senior Scout literature.

(2) A general knowledge of the social needs of the community in his neighbourhood and ability to find service for his Rovers.

(3) A personal standing, character and experience of life, such as will enable him to lead young men, and an understanding of the principles of leadership involved.

(4) Acceptance by the Rovers of the Crew concerned.

(5) Age sufficient to enable him to carry out the work satisfactorily. D.C.s and L.A.s are expected to consider carefully the suitability of the applicant in this respect, and particularly in relation to the ages of the members of the Crew. An applicant for a warrant as R.S.L. must be at least 25 years of age, and preferably 30; and as A.R.S.L. at least 21, and preferably 25 (P.O.R. 250).

The claims of National Service, which takes away most young men at 18 years of age, weigh heavily on the Rover section of the Movement, and the majority of Rover Crews are small in numbers. The hard-pressed G.S.M. may perhaps be excused if he seeks to fill vacancies for Scouters in the other sections first. But if the Group retains a large number of its Senior Scouts until they reach Rover age, there is everything to be said for a strong Rover Crew, and it will need suitable leaders. As regards the majority of Crews, consisting of three or four Rovers (some of whom may also be Scouters), manpower can perhaps be saved if the Rovers usually meet on a District basis, under the leadership of an Assistant Commissioner for Rovers or a District Rover Scout Leader. In such cases, the functions of one of the Rovers in each Crew as Rover Mate of that Crew are more important.

I need hardly say that warrants in the Rover section are not issued to ladies (P.O.R. 249).

Warrants

The G.S.M. is responsible for submitting applications for warrants as Scouters in his Group to the D.C. and L.A., and it is impossible to stress too strongly the importance of taking extreme care to check the credentials, and to ensure the suitability, of candidates. The character of those who have been boys in the Group will be well known to the G.S.M., and in their cases he will be mainly concerned with their suitability for the warrant which is being applied for. But when an outsider offers his services, the position is very different. We must not close our eyes to the plain fact that some very undesirable characters try to get into the Scout Movement.

P.O.R. 72 should really be known by heart by all G.S.M.s: —

"In view of the responsibility to parents and of the dangers which have been found to exist, L.A.s and D.C.s must take every precaution to ensure that no one whose moral character is open in any way to suspicion should be admitted into the Movement, and they must show no false mercy in any case where such a person has gained admission. When circumstances indicate that a criminal offence may have been committed, the D.C. must see that the police are informed."

First, then, the G.S.M. must not put forward the name of anyone of whose moral character he is not fully satisfied, nor must he allow any such person to associate with the boys. Not only must he talk with the applicant and satisfy himself that he fully accepts the moral principles of the Scout Movement, but he must also ask for references and follow them up—references from people who know the applicant well, and have known him for many years. One of the worst cases I can recall was a man who supplied excellent references, but it was not noticed that none of the referees had known him for more than five years. In due course, when the man was sentenced to prison for offences against boys, it was found it was just over five years since he came out of prison for similar offences.

These precautions apply not only to applicants for warrants, but to anyone who will be mixing with the boys, such as Instructors. Beware of the man who says he doesn't want to bother about a warrant!

Now we come to P.O.R. 73: —

"(i) Where any person whose character and past history are not fully known makes an offer of service, or seeks to be associated in any way with the Movement or any member of it as such, the matter must immediately be reported to the D.C., who will at once consult I.H.Q., using for this purpose, whenever possible, form WE, which is of 'Business Reply Envelope' design.

"(ii) In the absence of the D.C. or any A.D.C., or in case of urgency, the Scouter in charge of the Group concerned must communicate direct with I.H.Q.

"(iii) I.H.Q. will furnish a confidential report; and where the enquiry comes from a person other than a Commissioner, will also inform the D.C."

This is not red tape. I.H.Q. has over the years compiled a long list of people who have got themselves into trouble, and can supply information (more often than you might think) which will have a vital bearing on the issue or non-issue of a warrant, or indeed the employment of the applicant in any capacity in the Movement.

In the case of a sponsored Group, the G.S.M. must of course satisfy himself in addition that the applicant is acceptable to the Sponsoring Authority.

The procedure for the issue of warrants by I.H.Q. on the recommendation of the D.C. and L.A. is fully set out in Rules 64-75, as well as for the cancellation, suspension or return of warrants in Rules 76-88, and need not be detailed here.

But G.S.M.s should bear in mind that D.C.s and L.A.s will require to be satisfied that the applicant for a warrant, "is fully fitted by character and previous history to be entrusted with the care of boys, and has, in particular: —

"(1) The necessary qualifications required by the rule relating to the rank in question (as set out above).

"(2) A full appreciation of the religious and moral aim underlying the scheme of Scouting.

"(3) Personal standing and character such as will ensure a good moral influence and sufficient steadfastness of purpose to carry out the work with energy and perseverance.

"(4) A willingness to avail himself of any facilities offered for training appropriate to his rank" (P.O.R. 69).

The applicant for a warrant should serve three months' probation in the actual rank for which the warrant is desired, but the G.S.M. must let the D.C. know about him at once (P.O.R. 68). In the case of a young man who has come up through the Group itself, it is often wise to see if arrangements can be made for him to do his probationary service in another Group. This not only provides him with a new experience, but may also make it easier for him to find his feet among boys who are strangers to him, rather than among those with whom he has grown up.

When the applicant has had a chance of seeing a little of Scouting, and before the three months' probation is over, the G.S.M. should make a point of having a quiet talk with him. This is the time to be satisfied about the applicant's attitude to Scouting, and not after a warrant has been issued. In view of the qualifications required by the rules, the G.S.M. should satisfy himself upon such points as the following: —

Why does he want to help Scouting?

Does he accept, without reservation, the principles of the Scout Movement, and particularly the Scout Law and Promise?

What is his personal position regarding "Duty to God"?

Has he read the necessary books ("Scouting for Boys," etc.)?

What previous experience has he had in working with boys?

What are his own tastes and hobbies?

An armchair and a cup of tea provide the right atmosphere for such a talk, and not a corner of the Scout Headquarters with boys howling their heads off within a yard or two!

When the G.S.M. is happy about the man, and has forwarded form G to the L.A. Secretary, both the District Commissioner and the warrants committee of the L.A. will no doubt wish to see the applicant before forwarding the form to I.H.Q.

In due course, the District Commissioner or his Assistant will arrange to present the warrant on a suitable public occasion, usually either at a meeting of the Troop (or Pack), a Local Association meeting, or a gathering of Scouters. Whichever it may be, the G.S.M. should make a point of being present and sharing in the welcome given to the new warrant-holder, who will be making or renewing the Scout Promise at the beginning of his new responsibilities.

We must return for a moment to P.O.R. 72 (quoted above). If the G.S.M. is so unfortunate as to discover that suspicion of immorality rests upon one of his Scouters, he must take action at once and not attempt to hush it up. His bounden duty is to report the matter at once to the District Commissioner, who has the responsibiliy of informing the police. In the meantime, the Scouter should be suspended, and instructed that he must have no dealings with any of the boys until the matter has been investigated. On no account should the G.S.M. attempt to turn himself into an amateur detective agency. It is the job of the police and we must follow their directions. Information should be given confidentially to the Sponsoring Authority, in the case of a sponsored Group.

The training of the Scouters

Before getting a warrant, a Scouter should have expressed his willingness to avail himself of any facilities offered for training (P.O.R. 69). As the Chief Scout has said, "Scouting is a boy's game, but a man's job," and it is up to the man to qualify himself for the job by every means available.

In some Counties, explanatory courses are run, by means of which the prospective Scouter can get a general idea of the aims and methods of the Scout Movement, before he commits himself to applying for a warrant.

Then there are preliminary courses, designed for the new Scouter, perhaps while he is serving his three months' probation, or for a Scouter who is changing over from one section to another.

Then there is the system of Wood Badge training which is fully explained in the pamphlet "The Training of Scouters," and which, when its three parts have been satisfactorily completed, entitles the Scouter to wear the Wood Badge round his neck and to be enrolled as a member of the 1st Gilwell Park Group. The British training centre at Gilwell Park is recognised internationally as the world centre for the training of Scouters.

The best Groups have established a tradition that each of their Scouters should go through a preliminary course when he gets his warrant, and a Wood Badge course within three years at most. It is, of course, easier to persuade him to do so if the G.S.M. has set the example. Particulars of courses available are advertised locally by the County training teams, and all Wood Badge Part II courses, whether held at Gilwell Park or at a County training centre, are announced in "The Scouter." There should be no excuse for not knowing that a course is being run.

Attendance at such courses will involve the Scouter in some expense, although they are economically run. While most Counties (and indeed I.H.Q., too) have some funds available for helping needy Scouters, they will naturally enquire first what the Group itself is doing to help. It is a good tradition for the Group to pay the expenses of all their Scouters who attend such courses. If a Scouter does not need the money and likes to pay it back into the Group funds, well and good. But such a system avoids embarrassment to the man who would otherwise find it difficult to go.

But these official courses are neither the beginning nor the end of a Scouter's training. It has already been mentioned that a young Scouter who has grown up in the Group will find great value in serving an apprenticeship in another Group. He will return with greater authority and new ideas. The G.S.M. will be constantly on the lookout for other opportunities for training for his Scouters. The meetings of the Group Council, to which we shall refer in the next chapter, are themselves a valuable training-ground. So are District Scouters' meetings, County Conferences, and the two-yearly national conferences. (A man may have to take his turn for them, as Counties are given a quota which they cannot exceed, but they try to give opportunities for all ranks and ages to attend in rotation.) The watchful Group will find no lack of means by which its Scouters can widen their experience.

Lastly, there is always reading. The main source of new experience is the Movement's own monthly magazine, "The Scouter," through which the Chief Scout and I.H.Q. can keep in touch with all Scouters, and new ideas and stunts can be circulated. Really, all Scouters should subscribe for personal copies of " The Scouter "—there is so much in it which is worth keeping for reference. I.H.Q. itself publishes a number of valuable textbooks, many of which are referred to in the Appendix, and the Scout Shop book list contains many others (see also Chapter 18, under " Libraries ").

Transfers of Scouters

Many people move from one place to another when they change jobs or get married, and we lose a number of good Scouters by a failure to operate simple machinery when such a thing happens.

When a Scouter leaves a District, the warrant he held in his own Group must, of course, be cancelled. When it is sent to the L.A. Secretary for this purpose, the G.S.M. should give a report on the Scouter, being quite frank about his service, and his capabilities for further service in his new District. If he can also give the Scouter's new address, it will be passed on to I.H.Q. with the warrant, and I.H.Q. will pass on the information. All too often warrants are returned to I.H.Q. endorsed with the word " Removed," but the new address is not given.

If you hear, before the D.C. tells you, that a newcomer seems to be wearing a Scout badge or to be knowledgeable about Scouting, make him welcome (but remember not to let him loose among the boys until you have made enquiries through the D.C. as to his past history). A bachelor in a new place may well be at a loose end and be only too glad to take up Scouting straight away. But a newly-married couple must be given time to get the carpets down and the pictures up. Nevertheless, keep in touch with them, even if they can't be active at once, and invite them to an occasional Group event. " Cast thy bread upon the waters: for thou shalt find it after many days."

When a Scouter moves abroad, particularly to one of the Dominions or Colonies, the world-wide coverage of Scouting shows its great value, and the G.S.M. should draw the Scouter's attention to it. If the Scouter applies, through the D.C., to the Overseas Commissioner at I.H.Q., he will get a letter of introduction to the Scout Headquarters of the Dominion or Colony, which he can present on arrival. But if he tells I.H.Q. well in advance the date of his arrival, and the ship or plane by which he is travelling, he may perhaps be met and given a prompt welcome—and the promise of a Scout job without delay. In my travels abroad, I met many British Scouters whose first practical experience of the world-wide Scout Brotherhood was the welcome they received on setting foot in a strange country.

CHAPTER 5

THE GROUP COUNCIL

IN the last chapter we considered the individual Scouters —recruitment, warrants, and so on. It is time to deal with the Scouters of the Group as a team—a team of friends who are well accustomed to working and playing together and whose worries are the common concern of all.

The team works through the Group Council. P.O.R. 201 says: —

" (i) Where the Group consists of two or more sections, the Scouters of the sections will meet regularly to discuss matters affecting the Group. Such meeting is called the 'Group Council.'

" (ii) The G.S.M. will be chairman of the Group Council."

We do not often use the word " must " in Scouting if we can avoid it, but the word " will " as used in this rule surely has the same effect. Just as in the Scout Law we say "A Scout is loyal," meaning that if the boy comes into the Scout Movement he accepts this law as binding upon him, so we Scouters accept P.O.R. as our guide to what we do, and where P.O.R. says " will meet," there is an obligation on us to do so.

Save, therefore, for the exceptional Groups which consist of one section only, a Group Council is compulsory. And it will meet regularly. How often it meets will depend, of course, upon the business to be done. We shall see later that there are many things to discuss, and it may well be that we shall need to meet once a month; certainly not less than once every two months.

I know of Groups without a G.S.M. where the Scoutmaster who is acting as G.S.M. says: " We don't need to have meetings; I often run into Akela at the end of her Pack meeting and we have a word about things." Maybe they do, but they can have little idea of the valuable things a Group Council can do if it does not meet, particularly the value of training Assistants, giving them experience and even listening to their views now and again.

But while the Scouters should actually meet regularly, it does not follow that they need sit round a table on hard chairs in a cold and draughty headquarters (but of course yours isn't!). The average number of Scouters per Group in this country is only five, and such a number can surely meet in comfort in the home of the G.S.M., or in various homes in rotation. Armchairs need not be forbidden, and cups of tea have been known to help the proceedings along.

It will help the G.S.M. if one of the Scouters acts as Secretary of the Council, to take notes and make a record of any decision reached. Our memories are pretty untrustworthy, and it helps if we have a record of what we decided one, two, or more months ago. Perhaps someone has a typewriter, or even a girl at the office who is interested enough in Scouting to type out the record. However informal the meetings are, keep a Minute Book and see it is written up directly after each meeting.

All the Scouters are members, down to the newest young Assistant Cubmaster—and I would also include those who are serving their three months' probation, for it is all good experience. But Instructors and lay members of the Group Committee are not members, and should not be invited to the meetings. On suitable occasions I would make two exceptions to this rule—first, the Sponsoring Authority, if he wants to say something to all the Scouters, or if there is to be a discussion on such a subject as Church parades on which his views will be necessary; second, the Group Treasurer, if the G.S.M. thinks that his presence might be useful when such a matter is being discussed as the annual budget.

The G.S.M. is the chairman of the Group Council.

Naturally so, for he is in charge of the Group as a whole and has the obligation of ensuring co-operation between the various sections. As Mr. Neate has written: " The G.S.M.'s prime duty to the boys is to inspire, encourage, counsel and help that team of Scouters, and to take counsel with them." Much of the success of a Group Council will depend upon the way in which he conducts the meetings. He should not be in such a hurry to get the thing over that discussion is scamped, or the junior Scouters are discouraged from making their contribution. Nor should he seek to impose his own views except by methods of tactful persuasion. Above all, neither he nor the Group Council should interfere with the Scoutmaster in his running of the Troop, nor with the functions of the Court of Honour or the Crew in Council. They are free to criticise, if their own section is being affected by what the Troop is doing (or failing to do), but it must be left to the G.S.M. and the Scoutmaster in private session to decide upon what should be done. And the same applies to the leaders of the other sections.

There will be no difficulty about this kind of thing if the Scouters are a " team of friends," as I called them at the beginning of this chapter, and if they always bear one question in mind: " How does this benefit the boys?"

The job of the Group Council is stated in the broadest terms in P.O.R.—". . . to discuss matters affecting the Group." The points that may come up are of infinite variety, and I can only give a broad indication as to the kind of things that are likely to need discussion from time to time: —

(i) If the Group does not already consist of all sections, what can be done to complete them?

(ii) Does the training in the Pack link satisfactorily with that in the Troop, and so on up to the Crew?

(iii) Is all the training progressive, particularly as regards " Duty to God "?

(iv) Problems of headquarters, such as their use by the

different sections, cleaning and repairs, decorations for Pack and Troop, Patrol and Six corners.

(v) Recruitment of boys, where there are vacancies.

(vi) Are there long waiting-lists of boys? If so, can a second Pack or Troop be started?

(vii) Arrangements and dates for going-up ceremonies from one section to another.

(viii) Arrangements for combined shows, such as the annual entertainment, parents' evenings or Christmas parties.

(ix) Arrangements for Church parades in a sponsored Group.

(x) Arrangements for annual Scout camps and Pack holidays, dates, site, equipment, etc.

(xi) Sharing of equipment by the sections.

(xii) Recommendations to the Group Committee in connection with the annual budget (any special expenditure needed by a section, the amount the boys are expected to raise, and so on).

(xiii) Subjects common to all sections such as road safety or health.

(xiv) Relationships with the Sponsoring Authority, the schools, the local Youth Committee.

(xv) Relationships wtih the District Commissioner and Local Association.

(xvi) Reports by section leaders as to their sections, including any useful critical comments (*e.g.* as to how ex-Cubs get on in the Troop).

(xvii) Boys who have left, and why.

(xviii) Analysis of the last census figures, and lessons to be drawn from them (see pages 101-102).

(xix) Announcements by G.S.M. (County or District events, alterations in P.O.R., new books, etc.).

(xx) Arrangements for Scouters to visit other sections.

This is a long list, but by no means exhaustive. It may serve as a useful guide to a new G.S.M., and at least it shows that a Group Council should never be short of business! A number of other matters will occur to the reader as he reads subsequent chapters.

The training value of the Group Council should always be borne in mind, even for those with a good deal of experience. The new Scouter in particular can get a tremendous amount of advice and help from his older colleagues, and perhaps unconsciously pick up many useful tips and the right attitude to his job. I am sure that many young Assistant Scouters are lost to the Movement because the older Scouters do not give enough thought to their training, or give them sufficient responsibility. A good Group is a breeding-ground for good Scouters, but too often the young ones get no training to speak of, and do little on Troop nights but fetch things for the S.M. or run an occasional game. The Group Council should attend to this point, suggesting to some that they might specialise on some subject and then take over full responsibility for it; to others that they might launch out from the parent Group and take on a Pack or Troop of their own. An analysis of the census figures for this country will show that there are a number of Groups with one Scouter to every four or five boys. What do they all do? And wouldn't they be happier and better employed by transferring to a Group which is short-handed?

The Group Committee will be dealt with in the next chapter, and we will reserve until then the relationship between that body and the Group Council.

Little need be said about the uniform of the Group Scouters beyond repeating what has been said about the G.S.M.'s uniform (pages 30-31), and will be said later about that of the boys (pages 78-79). An example of smartness is essential. Uniforms may be old, but they can be neat and clean, and suitable to the ages and figures of the wearers. An occasional eccentricity on the part of a young Scouter may need checking—shorts rolled well up to the thigh, a scarf worn underneath the shirt collar, for example. Ladies need to be specially careful, in a boys' Movement, not to ape the masculine, nor, on the other hand, to deck themselves in frills, furbelows or fur coats. A mere male G.S.M. can refer them to the I.H.Q. pamphlet "Notes for Women Scouters," and, if need be, invoke the help of the Assistant Commissioner for Cubs or another Cub Scouter.

It is the usual custom, and the wish of the Chief Scout, that Scouters who have been honoured with King's or Queen's medals, war medals, decorations or orders shall wear the ribbons on their Scout uniforms. They are worn on the left breast, as distinct from Scout award emblems, which are worn on the right. A number of other authorised decorations will be found in P.O.R. 358. In loyalty to that rule, Scouters should be careful not to wear any decorations which are not authorised. Our wives or other female attachments who sew all the bits and pieces on our uniforms will be glad that there is a limit to their number.

Service Stars take a page and a half of P.O.R. (359-367), but for Scouters the rule is that they are optional. Here is a matter where uniformity within the Group is desirable, and if there are differences among the Scouters of your Group, the Group Council might well resolve them.

CHAPTER 6

THE GROUP COMMITTEE

"SCOUTING is a training in citizenship, and the help and sympathy of men and women in all walks of life are necessary if Scouting is to have its roots well down into the social life of the community which it seeks to serve."

For many years that excellent advice was not followed, except in a few enlightened places. Far too many Scouters built a wall round themselves and their Troops, and then complained that the community was not interested in Scouting. Of course the community wasn't interested; it wasn't given the chance.

There are still some Scouters who enjoy being a "one-man band," as the Manpower Report called them, and resent—or perhaps fear—any kind of interference, as they describe it, from outside. But they are now a small minority, and the average Scouter values the lay help which he receives, even if he doesn't always make the best use of it.

The centre of lay activity in the Group is the Group Committee, sometimes quite wrongly called the Parents' Committee. For nearly all Groups a Group Committee is compulsory, and we ought not to tolerate much longer those Groups which refuse or neglect to establish one. It is true that cases have arisen where a Group Committee has been a failure, but the failure is nearly always due to one or both of two causes. Either their functions have not been properly explained to the members at the outset, and they have assumed more power than they are given by our rules, or the G.S.M. has unwisely included in the membership one or two dominating personalities who have caused trouble. But these are exceptions, and care at the beginning should avoid such troubles. They form no valid excuse for refusing to have such a Committee, which, when properly used, can be a tower of strength.

I.H.Q. publish a good pamphlet called "The Group Committee." Much of the material in this chapter comes from it, and a copy should be on the table of every G.S.M., and supplied to every member of a Group Committee.

Membership

It is among the duties laid upon a G.S.M. that he should form a Group Committee (P.O.R. 173(4)), and that he should serve upon it (not sit on it, as a wag once said) himself. This applies wherever any money is received from outside the boys' own efforts, or where the Group has any property or equipment of its own. To all intents and purposes, this makes the formation of a Committee necessary in every Group, for there can be few that have no equipment!

P.O.R. 202 states that the Committee should be "composed of parents of the *Scouts,* representatives of the Old Scouts Branch, and others interested in the Group." It should certainly not be composed of parents only, and that is why it is so wrong to describe it as a Parents' Committee. The number of members should be workably small, but not so small as to exclude useful people. Perhaps eight may be regarded as a minimum, and I would myself try not to exceed twelve. Parents should include fathers and mothers of Cubs as well as Scouts. Old Scouts are always useful, especially as a link with the Group's Old Scout Branch, for their affection for their old Group is an abiding one. It is difficult to be precise as regards the "others interested," except to say that they should be chosen for their usefulness. If, for example, the Group is planning to build their own Headquarters, such people as a solicitor, a builder and a carpenter may be invaluable. Men and women who enjoy organising social events, or would act as box-office manager for the Group show, or enjoy editing a Group magazine, are always valuable. The G.S.M. must use his judgment in choosing those who are most useful in the circumstances of his Group at the time.

Although the rule is silent on the point, experience shows that it is wiser not to appoint members for an indefinite period, but to re-appoint them from year to year, or every two or three years, or to provide that one-third shall retire each year in rotation. From time to time the Group may need people with different qualifications. If parents of *Scouts* who have grown up and left the Group continue to be members, there may not be room for parents of new *Scouts*. In any case, new blood should be introduced regularly.

Members of the Group Committee are appointed or retired by the G.S.M., but he must get the approval of the D.C. and L.A. In the case of a sponsored Group, courtesy and wisdom alike demand that the G.S.M. should consult the Sponsoring Authority before putting names forward. It is asking for trouble not to do so. Indeed, particularly in the case of a Church-sponsored Group, it is wise to ask the Sponsoring Authority whether he could find time to serve on the Committee himself, or at least to nominate two or three representatives of the congregation to do so.

As we shall see when we come to examine the duties of the Group Committee, the members are there to work with, and under the direction of, the G.S.M. They must, therefore, be people with whom he can work comfortably and in whom he has confidence.

It is vital to the success of a newly-appointed Committee that they should understand their relation to the G.S.M., and not get the idea that they are there to run him and everybody else connected with the Group. They are in no way concerned with the actual training of the *Scouts* or with managing an Old Scout Branch (P.O.R. 202 (iii)). They should be quite clear in their minds that, whatever their individual views may be, Scouting is non-political, and that open Groups welcome *Scouts* of all denominations of religion and of none. It is not always easy for a G.S.M., especially if he is younger than many members of the Committee, to avoid giving an impression that he is trying to boss the show too much. For this reason, it is very valuable if the District Commissioner can be asked to attend the first meeting of a Group Committee, and to explain to the members what their duties are, and particularly what they are not. A further visit by the D.C. would also be valuable when there is a change of G.S.M.

Duties

What, then, are the duties of a Group Committee? P.O.R. 202 (i) is explicit on that point. The Committee is formed "to be responsible for Group property, and to assist the G.S.M. with finance, propaganda, and obtaining accommodation, camping grounds, and employment for the members of the Group, and in relation to the recognition, and the activities, of any body of parents, supporters, or other persons, engaged in any undertaking for or on behalf of the Group or any section of the Group."

That is a very long and legally-worded sentence, and we had better split it up and consider it in instalments. Note, first, that their duty is to assist the G.S.M. in all matters, except one. The exception is that they are themselves responsible for Group property, and if I were a G.S.M. I should be very glad that they are.

Now matters so important as Group property, finance and propaganda demand more space than this chapter affords, and will be deferred to the next. It is probably pretty rare for members of Group Committees to go out on the search for camping grounds—and the wise G.S.M. would certainly want to inspect their discoveries very carefully if they did, but it is a good thing for them to be aware of all the needs of the Group and to be alert in trying to satisfy them.

Employment for members of the Group was no doubt

included before "full employment" became a catchword for all political parties, but it is well that it should remain there, for at any time employment may become difficult to obtain. Moreover, members of the Committee may themselves be employers, or closely connected with those who are, and they may well be glad to offer vacancies and good opportunities for advancement to well-trained Scouts.

Let me add two or three more duties which I hope that all Group Committees will carry out. First, to be missionaries for Scouting to their own circles of friends and business associates. Secondly, to feel responsible for the continuity of the Group. Too many Groups or sections fall through when an individual Scouter retires, and it should be the duty of the Group Committee to see that this does not happen. Hence, they should always be on the alert for prospective Scouters. Thirdly, in view of what has been said on pages 35-36 as to the value of Instructors, members of the Committee should keep their eyes open for them, too. Perhaps in some cases the members might volunteer themselves if they realised that they were wanted. Fourthly, they should help the G.S.M. by acting as liaison with other local people—such people as ministers of religion, schoolmasters, youth organisers and members of other organisations, whom they may happen to know better than the G.S.M. does.

Such are the corporate duties of the Committee, but the G.S.M. will certainly hope that individual members may undertake particular jobs, and so relieve the Scouters. Some of these jobs may involve some work throughout the year; others will be connected with special events and will be wound up as soon as the events have occurred. These jobs are of great variety, such as quartermaster (or keeper of the equipment), manager of the Group headquarters, foreman of the labour gang, social leader, organiser of special events, chairman or secretary of ladies' sub-committee, librarian, editor of Group magazine or news-sheet, box-office manager.

Meetings

Many Group Committees in the past have been ineffective, and their best members have lost interest, because they have not met regularly or been given enough to do. It is hoped that the duties outlined above will keep the members occupied as much as their time will allow, but it is necessary for them to feel a corporate existence by meeting regularly. How often depends, as in the case of the Group Council, upon the kind of Group it is, and whether the requirements for money are many or few. Certainly, a Group Committee which is planning a new headquarters and raising the money for it will need to meet once a month, except perhaps in August and December. In other cases, once in two or three months may well be enough.

At whatever interval it seems necessary to meet, see that meetings are regular and fixed well in advance, preferably on a fixed day in the month, such as the last Wednesday, so that members may form the habit of keeping the evening free. Even so, they will not attend unless they can expect a good agenda, so that it is worth their while to turn out.

Meetings will tend to be more formal than those of the Group Council, and the numbers attending will probably make it inconvenient to hold them in private houses. But reasonable comfort and as much informality as possible may well be expected. Punctuality and briskness in conducting the business will be appreciated. If possible, agendas should be circulated in advance, and be accompanied by the minutes of the previous meeting.

Scouters, other than the G.S.M., are not members of the Committee and should not attend meetings as a body. It is a quaint custom of Scouters to talk in technical language, with much use of initials and abbreviations, and they are bound sooner or later to indulge in these mysteries, to the confusion and boredom of the lay members. But there may be occasions when it is useful for one of the section leaders to be invited to attend and speak on some item on the agenda. This will most often happen when the annual budget is being prepared and some unusual item of expenditure is being requested, such as the purchase of new tents or a camp abroad. Otherwise, the G.S.M. acts in liaison between the Group Council and the Group Committee, and keeps the two bodies in touch with one another.

The Officers of the Committee

The Committee needs a Chairman, a Secretary and a Treasurer. What manner of men should they be, and what are their duties?

Our rules are careful to say that "the G.S.M. will be a member of the Group Committee" (P.O.R. 202 (ii)), and not that he will be the Chairman. I know that many G.S.M.s prefer to be in the chair, on the grounds that they know better than anyone else what is to be discussed and that the business can be conducted more efficiently. Personally, I am against this view, as a general rule. It is very necessary to avoid any impression in the minds of members that their only duty is to be "yes-men," and this danger will be much less likely to arise if the G.S.M. is not in the chair. Again, the chairmanship of the Committee gives an opportunity of bringing in an influential layman, and winning his interest and often his enthusiasm for the Group. Indeed, I have known instances where a man has started in Scouting by being Chairman of a Group Committee and has later become a G.S.M.—and a very good one, too. Lastly, the G.S.M. has a freer hand, if he is not in the chair, to intervene when he feels it is necessary and to argue against some proposition. You cannot do a good job as Chairman if you are at the same time involved in a (perhaps heated) argument.

For a Chairman, we should look for a man of standing and experience of affairs, who will conduct the meetings without fumbling or nervousness. In order to do that, he will be available to the G.S.M. and the Secretary, so as to be in touch with current affairs and know what is on the agenda. In other words, he will be more than a nominal Chairman, and the G.S.M. should be able to look to him for wise advice at any time. Such a man takes a little finding, but the search is well worth the trouble, if you get the right man in the end.

Similarly, neither the Secretary nor the Treasurer should be one of the Scouters, who have plenty of other things to do. The Secretary is one of those patient souls who are prepared to do the humdrum jobs which fall to any Secretary. Fortunately, there are many people who like that kind of work, and do it punctually and methodically. Many will be found among the ranks of women—perhaps an ex-Cubmaster whose age or family ties prevent her from running a Pack but whose interest in Scouting is unabated. The Secretary calls the meetings which have been arranged, circulates the agenda as agreed with the Chairman and G.S.M., keeps the minutes and circulates copies of them if that is the Committee's custom, and drafts the report for the Group's annual meeting (which is dealt with on page 181). I like to think that he may also be able to help the G.S.M. with some of his correspondence, but that depends upon whether he can persuade the G.S.M. to hand any over! Our poor reputation for not answering letters should be refuted by any efficient Group.

A specimen agenda for a Group Committee might read as follows: —

1. Chairman's welcome to new members.
2. Apologies for absence.
3. Minutes of last meeting (to be taken as read if previously circulated).
4. Matters arising from the minutes.
5. Treasurer's report.
6. G.S.M.'s report, including the activities of the sections (but kept quite brief).

7. Correspondence.
8. Main items for consideration (to be described, so that members know the main things for discussion).
9. Any other business (if accepted by the Chairman).
10. Date of next meeting (or, perhaps better, dates for the next two meetings).

It is an excellent custom to start each meeting with a prayer, or if any member cannot by the rules of his religion join in prayer with those of other faiths, to stand for a short period of silence, during which each member offers up his own petition.

The Secretary's duties have been aptly summed up by Mr. A. D. Macdonald in the following verse: —

" If your members of Committee turn up gladly,
And you've something good they're eager to discuss;
If your meetings are conducted with good humour,
But with well-defined objective, and no fuss;
If your Minute Book reflects the Group's endeavour
With correctness, but with brevity and wit;
If you've helped to place a job with every member,
THEN—as Secretary to the Group—you're IT."

The duties of the Treasurer are pretty obvious, aren't they? He must be a man who likes keeping accounts, and gets a thrill out of balancing his books at the first attempt, but has patience enough to find out where the mistakes are if (as usually happens) they don't! I believe that Bank Managers are thought to be a good line, and they certainly have the qualifications, but those I know are Treasurers of so many funds that I doubt whether they really have the time to take a sufficiently detailed interest in a Group's accounts. The good Treasurer has to be in touch with the section leaders as well as with the G.S.M., and may well have to show them what they have to do, for some of them (as the Headquarters pamphlet says) are " unbusinesslike and slipshod." But we will defer this point until Chapter 7.

Parents' and Supporters' Associations

As the years have gone by, many well-established Groups have gathered round them a host of lay people who are interested in the welfare of the Group and like to have some definite connection with it. They cannot all be members of the Group Committee, and the custom has grown up of forming a separate body, which may be known as a Parents' Association or a Supporters' Association, or some other patent name invented by the Group. Now this is an excellent thing, for the more people who are connected with Scouting the better, and it by no means follows that a parent's interest in the Group ceases when his boy grows old enough to leave. I would do everything to encourage a much larger number of such bodies, and get as many people as possible to become members, perhaps paying a small annual subscription of 2s. 6d. or so, but certainly pledged to run some money-raising efforts and social events each year.

But their relationship with the Group's official lay body, the Group Committee, must be made clear from the start, and this is where trouble has sometimes arisen in the past. Now P.O.R. has laid it down that such a body is responsible to the G.S.M. and the Group Committee. This is what is meant by the legal language of P.O.R. 202 (i): ". . . to assist the G.S.M. . . . in relation to the recognition, and the activities, of any body of parents, supporters, or other persons, engaged in any undertaking for or on behalf of the Group or any section of the Group." Speaking as a Group Treasurer myself, I can testify that this is easy to arrange, provided that it is done when the body is set up, and not suddenly imposed upon it when it has got into its stride. The Parents' Association, as many call it, has its own Chairman, Secretary and Treasurer, who run its own Committee, but that Committee is invited to send two representatives to the Group Committee, and the Group Committee in turn is invited to send representatives to the Committee of the Parents' Association. The Association runs a number of money-raising events each year, but pay the proceeds over to the Treasurer of the Group Committee, and all their receipts and expenses are incorporated in the Group's accounts.

Differences of opinion

We should not readily assume that such differences of opinion as are bound to arise will lead to loss of temper or a heated dispute. Nearly all such differences get themselves settled quite amicably and are quickly forgotten, for most people are friendly and sensible, and remember that they are in the Scout Movement for the benefit of the boys.

But P.O.R. provides a recognised procedure for use when necessary.

P.O.R. 202(iv): "In the case of any difference of opinion between the Group Committee and the Group Council the matter must be referred to the L.A. and D.C." By which I take the rule to refer only to differences of opinion which cannot easily be settled within the Group by the G.S.M.

P.O.R. 202(v): "In the event of any difference of opinion between either the Group Committee or Group Council and any body of parents, supporters, or other persons, engaged in any undertaking for or on behalf of the Group or any section of the Group, the matter must at once be referred to the L.A. and D.C."

The words "at once" are important and might well be included in P.O.R. 202 (iv) also, for it is unfair to the L.A. and D.C. if they do not hear about the dispute until tempers have had time to rise and opinions have become obstinately unalterable.

The G.S.M.'s encouragement

It will pay heavy dividends if the G.S.M. gives every encouragement to members of the Group Committee. Some of them have boys of their own in the Group; all may be expected to be interested in the boys for whom they are working. But so often they get no opportunities of seeing those boys. They should always receive invitations to suitable functions, such as the Group entertainment, handcraft exhibition or parents' evenings, and not to be left to find out these events for themselves. The last-named occasions are specially useful, for they can there meet not only the boys but also the parents, and may even gather some candid comments upon the work of their Committee.

Individual members might be invited by the section leaders to drop in at their convenience at a Pack or Troop meeting.

If the annual Troop camp is not too far away, the Group Committee will welcome an invitation to spend a day there, and its members can often provide transport. The ladies particularly are greatly intrigued at the sight of the boys cooking, and often genuinely surprised at its quality when they come to sample it.

The point is that they like to feel they are part of the show, and are made welcome when they join in. They will carry on their work with renewed enthusiasm as a result.

I am a great believer in the Supporter's Badge, which the G.S.M. can present to members of Group Committees and other supporters who are not members of the Movement (P.O.R. 400-401). Although the possession of the badge does not confer membership of the Movement, it is greatly appreciated and regularly worn by the proud recipients. Many of these people like to be allowed to take the Scout Promise, and the G.S.M. will be wise to make this known.

Lastly, I would mention the Thanks Badge (see page 203).

CHAPTER 7

THE GROUP'S MONEY

NOW for the Group's money, or, if yours is a very wealthy Group, " finance." The general principle is stated in P.O.R. 17, namely that Groups are expected to support themselves locally. Although in certain circumstances, which will be mentioned later, grants may be obtainable for special projects, the Movement has rightly been proud of its independence, and long may it continue! We can, I am sure, claim to be less dependent upon outside help than any other youth movement, and it is part of the training of our *Scouts* to maintain independence and thrift. Our aim is to raise what we need, by the boys themselves as far as possible, and to have a bit over to help those less fortunate than ourselves.

Under P.O.R. 208, the Group Committee and its Treasurer are responsible for managing the funds of the Group and, under P.O.R. 210, the G.S.M. must see that accounts of all moneys are kept. We are receiving money from boys, parents and supporters and the public, and we owe it to them that it should be scrupulously accounted for.

Let us hope that the time is past when a Scoutmaster can keep Scout money mixed up with his own, and that no Treasurer, entering on his office, will be confronted with the situation in which I was placed when I entered the Movement in that humble capacity. Perhaps I may be permitted this personal reminiscence as an awful warning to the present generation. It was in 1918 that I found myself on a holiday close by the field where the Troop from home, of which I knew little or nothing, was holding its summer camp. I saw a lot of them, and liked the Scouts' good order and friendliness. Just as they were leaving, I rashly asked the Scoutmaster whether I could give the Troop any help when we got back to London, expressly disclaiming any intention of learning such mysteries as knotting, signalling or first-aid. The Scoutmaster, in a flash, asked me whether I would keep the Troop accounts. Relieved at so easy an assignment, I agreed, and when I next met him, I enquired as to the accounts which I was to keep. The "accounts" proved to be a number of scraps of paper. The Scoutmaster told me he had been doing a bit of figuring, and reckoned he owed the Troop about £7. After examining the waste paper handed over, and doing a bit more figuring, I reckoned the Troop owed him about £8! The difference of £15 staggered him. I made a lot of enquiries, but it was quite by accident that I discovered that the Vicar had been given £15 to guard, several years before, but the Scoutmaster had forgotten all about it.

I hope I may be pardoned for this digression, but the story may have a moral, even to-day, for some unbusiness-like Groups.

The time is also past when a Scout Group can be run on about 2½d. a year. We can run a Group much more cheaply than almost any other organisation that attempts so varied a programme, but at present levels of prices any Group requires to raise quite a lot of money if it is going to give its members the full *Scout* programmes. Uniforms which were about 12s. 6d. to 15s. complete in my early days are now about £3, and a Patrol tent costs over £20.

That is where the Group Committee and the Treasurer come in, and relieve the Scouters of a grave burden.

Raising the money

The first thing the Group Committee wants to know is how much the Group will need to spend in the year. Not until then can they plan how they will raise the necessary funds.

Very early in their financial year, therefore, they will want to prepare a budget for that year, as the Chancellor of the Exchequer does for his National Group. It is a tremendous advantage if the Treasurer is able to present them with his accounts for the previous year very soon after it ends. They are usually quite simple accounts, and need not cause much work, provided that they can be made to balance, and that the books have been kept written up to date.

It is usually arranged that the G.S.M. meets his Group Council and asks the section leaders to give him their estimates of what they will need during the year. Many of the items vary little, and can be estimated at the amount spent during the previous year. It is the exceptional items, or those that recur only at intervals, which need special attention—such as the renewal of one or more tents, or the redecoration of the headquarters. The section leaders should also be able to say how much their boys ought to be able to raise during the year.

When these figures have been agreed by the Group Council, the G.S.M. and the Treasurer will be well advised to study them together and reach agreement before presenting them to the Group Committee for adoption. Tact and persuasion may sometimes be required, for some Treasurers are notoriously reluctant to spend money, and Group Councils have been known to pitch their demands too high.

The Group Committee is now in a position to see where it stands, knowing how much it has in hand at the beginning of the year, how much the boys may be expected to earn, and how much the expenditure is expected to be. Assuming that it would like to carry forward at the end of the year a balance approximately equal to that brought forward at the beginning, the difference is the amount the Group Committee must itself raise during the year, with the help of the Parents' or Supporters' Association, if there is one. The members are usually very amiable about it, I find, if the figures have been properly presented to them, but are not always so accommodating if they are given no proper details, but are just told that they are expected to raise a certain sum.

It is a good principle that the boys should raise as much as possible, for it is part of their training. There will be their own weekly subscriptions, their earnings in " Bob-a-job " week (as to which more later) and such money-raising efforts as the Group show (by whatever name called), sales of handcraft, and so on. Admittedly, this is much easier where the Group is well established and there is a good proportion of boys of some experience, and the Group Committee will be wise to bear this in mind when the Group is new or in process of re-formation, and be prepared to take upon their own shoulders a greater weight of the burden for a few years. But even in a new Group, " Bob-a-job " week gives an opportunity, which was denied before its invention, for the young *Scouts* seem to collect jobs more easily than the older ones. The Group Committee will, in most cases, be wise to accept the view of the G.S.M. and the Group Council as to the amount which the *Scouts* can reasonably be expected to earn in the year, for the Scouters are in the best position to judge.

As to the balance which the Group Committee must raise, it must be said at once that there is no objection in principle to their asking for subscriptions and donations from their supporters and well-wishers. This is sometimes misunderstood. P.O.R. 19(i) states: " The spirit of the Movement is that, *on the part of the boys themselves,* money should be earned and not solicited." (The italics are mine.) It does not say, and never has said, that adults must not solicit money. There are many people who are genuinely keen on Scouting, but do not actively participate in it, and they are very willing to subscribe if asked to do so. (There are, of course, objections to general appeals, and more will be said about that under the heading of " Unsuitable methods " below.) But in addition to obtaining subscriptions, it will probably be necessary to raise some money by other means—social events, such as dances or whist drives (but these are not everywhere approved of), sales of work, fun fairs and Christmas markets.

Wherever possible, an attempt should be made to avoid having to raise an unusually large sum in one year. An unexpected emergency may sometimes make it unavoidable, but intelligent anticipation, particularly on the part of the G.S.M. and the Group Council, can help a great deal. They know that tents wear out, that Group headquarters need repair and redecoration, that plans for increasing the size of the Group will require more equipment in a year or two. If funds are so arranged that a surplus can be budgeted for when there are no special demands for money, such a surplus can be carried forward as a reserve for use when the heavy expenditure occurs in a future year.

Plans for building a new headquarters demand special consideration, and will be dealt with in Chapter 8. Except for such special plans, the Group Treasurer should not seek to hoard money. Each generation of boys (and indeed of Group Committee members) should bear its share in the raising of money.

Unsuitable methods

The Scout Law sets a high standard for boys to live up to, and it is a help to them if their parents and supporters set themselves a higher standard in regard to methods of raising money than others do. It pays dividends, too, in the long run, in the respect in which Scouting will be held by the community. While it is the duty of the G.S.M. under P.O.R. 207 to ensure that no undesirable methods of raising money are employed, it is also an implied obligation upon members of Group Committees and Parents' Associations to be equally scrupulous. For this reason, they should be made fully aware of the provisions of P.O.R. 17-21.

P.O.R. 17: "No unit may make any appeal for funds, or otherwise attempt to raise money, in any area outside its own." No explanation seems to be required. No one wants to cause confusion or ill-feeling. But the rule would not have been put into the book if such invasions of territory had not occurred thoughtlessly.

P.O.R. 18: " Groups are not allowed to issue any form of general appeal for funds, unless permitted by the L.A. and D.C. in exceptional circumstances. In giving such permission, the L.A. and D.C. must designate the exact area in which the appeal may be made, which must not in any event overstep the boundaries of the L.A. itself." Again, this is just common sense. The Scout Movement does not want to get the reputation of being a begging society. At the same time, it may happen that one Group in a District may be raising a big sum to build a headquarters, while the other Groups in that District have no exceptional needs at that time. The L.A. and D.C. are the best people to judge whether a general appeal by one Group would be objected to, and would no doubt consult the G.S.M.s of the other Groups before giving permission. But they are only responsible for a particular area, and cannot commit the Scout people outside that area.

P.O.R. 19 (i) has been mentioned earlier, and embodies a vital principle. " The spirit of the Movement is that, on the part of the boys themselves, money should be earned and not solicited." The G.S.M. must be adamant about this. Under no circumstances must boys ask for money. There were times when small boys would arrive on a man's doorstep with collecting cards—but not now, I hope. There is, of course, no objection to boys selling tickets to their friends and neighbours for the Group show, because they are giving value for money (one devoutly hopes), but any general house-to-house visitation, to people the boys do not know, must be ruled out.

P.O.R. 19 (ii) deals with the acceptance of grants, and has a piece to itself later in this chapter.

P.O.R. 20: " *Scouts* must not take part in street sales or collections, either for their own funds or for other institutions or charities, nor in any method of touting the public, but they may assist institutions or charities as messengers or in other capacities. They may also assist under proper supervision in the selling of programmes at a fixed price at recognised entertainments." Group Committees must bear this in mind when arranging shows for Group funds. Invitations by outside bodies to do things of this kind will usually go direct to the G.S.M. or section leader, and can be more conveniently dealt with under "Good Turns" (see pages 136-137).

P.O.R. 21: "All members of the Movement, acting as such, must observe the provisions of Rule 20, and must not countenance or be concerned in any public method of raising money for *Scout* or other purposes which is in any way contrary to the law of the land, or likely to encourage *Scouts* in the practice of gambling." This is the point at which trouble is most likely to arise. In these days of football pools and raffles, someone on the Group Committee is pretty sure to say, "Why not have a raffle (or draw, or whatever you like to call it)?" And indeed, why not, if you adopt the standard of the world around you? But we really are quite clear in our minds, are we not, that the standard set by the Scout Law is not the standard of the world around us? So let us cut these things out, and earn our money the harder way. When people say that there is no harm in a little raffle, our answer is, I think, twofold: (i) nearly all raffles are against the law of the land, even if the police happen to take no action in a particular case; (ii) it is almost impossible to ensure that none of the *Scouts* buy tickets. If they do, are we not encouraging them in the practice of gambling? On both counts, Rule 21 will find us guilty if we run these affairs.

The Group's Accounts

I shall not be tempted to tell Group Treasurers what kind of accounts they should keep. No standard form is imposed upon them, because Headquarters believe that a Treasurer will get on best if he keeps the kind of accounts which suit him and which are adapted to the circumstances of his Group. All I would beg is that they should be understandable to him, to his successor, and to the members of the Group Committee, who may not be so accustomed to reading accounts as he is. It should also be borne in mind that any member of the Group is, under P.O.R. 210, entitled to inspect them.

The accounts of most Groups can be very simple, and do not necessitate any elaborate system of double-entry. If they did, some of us would be disqualified from being Treasurers. A simple income and expenditure account, together with a list of assets, is normally adequate.

It is important that the accounts should include all the money transactions of the Group, including the receipts and expenses of the G.S.M., the section leaders and the Parents' Association. It is, I think, the usual custom for the section leaders to receive the *Scouts'* weekly subscriptions, and they certainly have to spend a number of small sums on odds and ends. These can be dealt with as explained below, but they should all be reported to the Treasurer and be included in his accounts.

The accounts are made up annually, to a regular date which the Group Committee is free to fix, but there is much to be said for choosing 31st March as the closing date, as this is the end of the Scout year for census and other purposes. They must be audited by an independent and responsible person (P.O.R. 210). The Treasurer will, it is hoped, have sufficient copies made so as to supply a copy to the G.S.M. and to each member of the Group Committee and, I would add, to each section leader. He will present them to the Group Committee at its first meeting after they are ready, together with a report on the main features. A copy of the accounts must be sent to the L.A. within four months of the end of the Group's accounting year (P.O.R. 211), and should be accompanied by a schedule of Group property (P.O.R. 206), as to which more will be said under the heading of "Insurance" on pages 94-96.

Under P.O.R. 208, all receipts except subscriptions paid by the *Scouts* themselves must be paid into a bank, Post Office Savings, or other similar account in the name of the Group operated by two members of the Group Committee. This is good business custom, and is a protection to the Treasurer against base insinuations! A bank account has advantages over the other forms of account permitted, in the case of drawing cheques, but where it happens that a Group possesses more cash than it is likely to need in the near future, there is merit in putting any such surplus into the Post Office Savings Bank, where it can earn a little interest. This particularly applies to a period of the year when the *Scouts* are paying weekly sums, often some months in advance, for their annual camp. The bank or other account should be in the name of the Group, and not of any individual, and two signatures should be required on cheques or notices of withdrawal. One signature will naturally be that of the Treasurer, while the other will be that of the G.S.M. or of a member of the Group Committee who is readily accessible.

Just as the receipts mentioned above should be paid into a bank or other account, so all large sums should be paid out by cheque.

It is impracticable to get the authority of the Group Committee before making every payment. In order to avoid such inconvenience, it is usual for the Group Committee to authorise the Treasurer to sign cheques up to a stated maximum, and to give similar authority to the G.S.M. and the section leaders to spend up to another stated maximum without the authority of the Treasurer. The Committee will be the more ready to give such authority if a properly thought out budget has been presented to it at the beginning of the year. If a large unexpected item of expense occurs, it is well to defer a decision upon it until the Committee has been consulted, but if time does not allow, at least the Treasurer must be consulted, for he will have to pacify the members at the next meeting.

The Scouters' petty cash

Under P.O.R. 209, "subscriptions paid by the *Scouts* themselves will be administered by the section concerned, as will also any sums allotted to the section for current expenses by the Group Committee in consultation with the Group Council. The accounts of section funds, if kept separately, will be included in the annual accounts of the Group."

As indicated above, each of the section leaders and the G.S.M. himself will be spending small sums of money on odds and ends from week to week, and will be receiving the *Scouts*' subscriptions. The Treasurer's job is to arrange a simple system under which the Scouters account to him for these receipts and expenses. The emphasis must be on the word "simple," for many of them will need some help with even the simplest form of bookkeeping. An ordinary single-column cash book is sufficient, in which the Scouter enters his receipts on one side and his expenditure on the other. The Treasurer will need to be forbearing in demanding receipts for expenditure incurred, and not expect them for such small sums as the purchase of stamps. But he has the right to expect receipts for larger sums, and it is for him to agree with the G.S.M. what the general rule should be.

It is probable that in most sections, current expenses will exceed receipts, and the Treasurer will need to advance the section leaders appropriate sums from time to time. It should therefore be arranged that, before the Scouter runs out of funds, he should hand in his cash book to the Treasurer, who can then extract a summary of the receipts and expenses and enter the figures in the Group account books, and hand the book back to the Scouter with whatever further advance is agreed to be reasonable. This may afford the Treasurer an opportunity of calling upon the Scouter at the Group headquarters, and seeing something of the boys.

It is an essential feature of Scouting that the *Scouts* themselves should be responsible for the expenditure of the funds allotted to them. These are defined in P.O.R. 209 as being the " subscriptions paid by the *Scouts* themselves " and " any sums allotted to the section for current expenses." The Sixers of the Cub Pack may be regarded as too young to take much responsibility in this respect, although the wise Cubmaster will start the training they will get later by consulting them on the money they will spend on, say, a Pack expedition. But the Court of Honour in the Boy Scout Troop and in the Senior Scout Troop, and the Crew Council in the Rover Crew, are given this responsibility under the rules (P.O.R. 239 (ii), 247L (ii) and 261 (i)), and the G.S.M. and the Scouters must take pains to see that they shoulder it.

The Treasurer can help by giving a simple talk once a year on the Group accounts, showing how the boys' own money has been spent and how much had to be raised by other means.

Boys' subscriptions

A few Groups charge a fairly large sum each week, and out of this weekly subscription meet the cost of uniforms and of camps. But the usual practice is to charge a low amount as the ordinary subscription, and to deal with uniforms and camps separately. No doubt the fixed subscription varies from Group to Group, but I believe that the usual amount is 1d. a week for Cubs, 2d. or 3d. a week for Boy Scouts, and perhaps a bit more for Seniors and Rovers.

I think that the G.S.M. would be wise to consider whether sums like that are not too low in present conditions, compared with what the boys pay for other things such as sweets, comics and visits to the pictures. Would they value Scouting more if it cost them a bit more? At the same time, we certainly don't want to make it difficult for any boy to remain in the Pack or Troop because it is too expensive. Perhaps a scheme known as the "self-assessment scheme" would work in many Groups, as it certainly has in some. This scheme involves the payment of a minimum subscription of about the amounts suggested above, and this is compulsory for everybody. But, in addition, the parents are asked by the G.S.M. or the Group Committee to consider, after their boy has been in the Pack or Troop a few weeks, how much he is enjoying his Cubbing or Scouting, and to pay an extra weekly (or monthly or quarterly) sum according to their means. The extra sum is entirely voluntary, and the amounts so paid are not known to the other boys. Groups that have tried this method have found that their income is very considerably increased. But, while Patrol Leaders collect the minimum subscriptions, it is necessary for an adult to collect the additional amounts, in order to keep them secret.

"Bob-a-job" week

During a week in April each year, the Chief Scout asks every boy and Scouter in the Movement to do some jobs for payment. The amounts so earned are collected by the Group, and 2s. per head is sent to Imperial Headquarters as a contribution towards their expenses. It seems likely that this will continue, for it is difficult to see how the work of Headquarters could be carried on without it, and in point of fact a considerably larger sum remains in Group funds each year. Indeed, "Bob-a-job" week has become a national institution, much publicised in Press and on the radio, and is received very cordially by the general public.

A few points in connection with it need to be watched by the G.S.M. and Group Committee. In the first place, these jobs must be done during the week announced by I.H.Q., and during that week only. We must not be tempted by the success of the week to repeat it for our own benefit at other times during the year. That would be contrary to the spirit of the *Scout* good turn, and might even land the Group in trouble with the law. The provisions of the Employment of Children Act are very strict, and Chief Constables who look benevolently on our efforts once a year might be less lenient if they found that the effort was being repeated in their areas.

Then, we must make it abundantly clear to our boys that, in return for the help of the public during that one week, they must do even more good turns for the other 51 weeks of the year. It is an excellent plan for a boy who has been paid for a job during " Bob-a-job " week to make another call a month later and offer to do a job for nothing.

The Treasurer will need to see that the money earned by the boys, and the job cards on which the earnings are recorded, are promptly accounted for, and not left lying in the boys' hands. Section leaders should collect the money and the cards directly the week is over, check the amounts and hand them over to the Group Treasurer, who enters the total amount in his books and pays the gross amount into the bank. As soon as all the cards are accounted for, he pays over to the Local Association Treasurer 2s. per head for each boy appearing on the Group census at the previous 31st March, together with any sums which are due, under agreed arrangements, to the County and the District. The remainder belongs to the Group, and a very useful addition to the funds it is. In some L.A.s, the total amount collected is paid over to the L.A. Treasurer, who refunds to the Group the amount it is entitled to keep.

Uniforms

It is a good principle for the Group to buy the boys' uniforms, in order that there may be uniformity. If it is left to the parents, all sorts of shades of khaki, grey, green or blue may appear, not to mention fancy jerseys knitted by fond Cub-mothers. But it is a bad principle for the Group to pay for the uniforms, for that is the responsibility of the parents.

The best arrangement is, I think, for the Scouter who

visits the parents, as he or she must surely do when a boy joins, to discuss the cost of uniform with them, and get their agreement to the Group's buying it. They can then be asked whether they are prepared to pay the full amount at once, or whether they would prefer to repay the Group by weekly instalments of agreed amounts. A scheme of this kind must, of course, be acceptable to the Group Committee, which must be prepared to keep the necessary funds free for the purpose. There is a risk of loss, I will admit, if the boy leaves before the instalments are paid up, but in my own experience losses are small, and the advantages of the scheme justify an allocation of funds.

While the general principle is that the parents pay, the Group should be prepared to give some help in special cases, as for example when the father has been sick and away from work or where the mother is a widow. Subscribers to the Group like to feel that their money may be used in such a way. It is best if the help is given privately, by arrangement with the Group Treasurer and without the boy knowing anything about it.

Camps

The small amounts needed for week-end camps are usually no great problem to the boy or his parents, but the summer camp, which may last for a fortnight and be held a long way away, is a different matter, and all Groups should be prepared to receive camp fees by convenient instalments.

Some Groups run a Thrift Fund into which boys can pay all the year round, and withdraw sums from it as they need them for summer camp or for their own holidays or what-not. In such a case, a separate Camp Fund will not be necessary. But in most cases it will be camp for which the boy wants to save, and the Group Committee should be prepared to open a Camp Fund about the beginning of January. This allows for a period of about 30 weeks before the usual time for summer camp, and materially helps the poorer boys to collect their camp fees in time. I think that the Scoutmaster usually collects the instalments on Troop nights, but it would certainly leave him freer to do his other jobs if the Group Treasurer or one of the Group Committee were prepared to come down and take the money.

Whoever collects it, it must be properly recorded each week, and the boy should be given a card on which the amounts he pays, and the total to date, are recorded week by week, and initialled by the recipient.

Deserving cases which need some help from the Group can be dealt with in the way suggested under "Uniforms" above.

During the period in which camp instalments are being most frequently paid in, it will be found that the Scoutmaster is accumulating quite a lot of money, and the Treasurer should see that any surplus over the amount usually allowed to the Scoutmaster for petty cash is paid over to Group funds. It can easily be drawn out when camp is approaching.

Scouters' expenses

Even in a well-organised Group, it is sometimes overlooked that the Scouters may be paying out of their own pockets expenses which should properly be met by the Group. But, as the Manpower Report said, "Personal expenses for uniform and books, for camping and minor travelling expenses, every Scouter expects to bear, for they are the normal expenses of his hobby. But no one should be expected to meet out of his own pocket expenditure which is proper to the Group Committee—such expenditure as the cost of postages or equipment for the Group, or extensive travelling expenses, especially in rural areas." If the Treasurer makes it clear to the Group Council that it is an understood thing that such expenses are reimbursed, no one need feel embarrassed at claiming them. And if they like to refund them to the Group, that is their affair.

Grants

The policy of the Scout Movement in regard to the

acceptance of grants from public bodies is laid down in P.O.R. 19 (ii): " Provided the Group or L.A. is responsible for raising a reasonable part of its funds, the acceptance of grant-aid is not contrary to the policy of this rule." But it is a good general rule that a Group should be as far as possible independent, and the great majority of Groups carry on happily from year to year without asking for, or expecting, a penny of grant-aid. Not only is this good Scout training, in days when everyone seems to be clamouring for public money, but it is the course of prudence also. Public policy changes, the amounts available for distribution may be drastically curtailed, and (although this has not happened up to the present) burdensome conditions may be imposed by the local authority.

The cases in which grant-aid is most easily justified are those in which a Group headquarters is being erected, and new Groups which are faced with heavy expenditure for initial equipment. Applications for capital grants of this kind need careful handling, and their success or failure may depend upon the way in which they are presented. Fortunately, the Grants Department at I.H.Q. is always ready to give advice on this subject, and I cannot stress too strongly that they should be consulted before any application for a capital grant is made. It must also be remembered that applications for grants from the Ministry of Education, Local Education Authorities or other bodies must be supported by the District Commissioner, while applications to I.H.Q. for grants from funds controlled by them must be approved both by the District and by the County Commissioner (P.O.R. 19 (ii)). This ensures a fair distribution of grants and prevents one Group from emptying the till!

(A Group in Scotland should know that the acceptance of grant-aid in that country is subject to a ruling of the Scottish Executive Committee, which should be ascertained from Scottish Headquarters before any application is even considered.)

The sources of grant-aid fall into two categories: (i) public money administered by the Education Authorities; and (ii) funds administered for special purposes by I.H.Q. Most grants under (i) can be more conveniently dealt with in the next chapter (pages 89-91), but it may be mentioned here that some Local Education Authorities are willing to make grants to Scouters towards the expenses of attending training courses, or to specially picked senior boys for attending Jamborees or making foreign visits. Each L.E.A. is a law unto itself in matters of grants, and it is wise to consult the District Commissioner, in order to find out the local practice.

As regards the special funds administered by I.H.Q., G.S.M.s and Group Treasurers should be aware that such funds exist. They are not large, and it is well to explore other sources of help before making application. They are as follows: —

King George V Jubilee Trust—see page 91.

Forster Memorial Fund—to assist Scouts in their career, with preference to Scouts of Surrey. Applications should be made by 30th June in each year. If no application from Surrey has been received by that date, those from other areas will be considered.

Treloar Handicapped Scouts Fund—to help crippled handicapped *Scouts* in institutions and in ordinary Groups.

Whitehead Bequest—to encourage the emigration of Scouts to the Dominions.

Migration Fund—to assist the emigration of Scouts to the Dominions under Agricultural Scholarships.

Poor Groups Fund—to help in obtaining essential equipment for new Groups and those serving poor boys.

A.O.F.B. Fund—to assist poor Scouts to go to camp.

Benevolent Fund—to assist members and ex-members of the Movement in genuine distress.

Sea Scout Funds—to aid Sea Scout Troops to obtain boats and equipment, and to aid the development of Sea Scout training.

Although no grant is repayable to I.H.Q., it has often been found that a Group which has been helped in this way has offered repayment, in whole or part, at a later date. Such offers are much appreciated, as they enable other Groups to receive help which might not otherwise be possible.

Income Tax

It is not possible to go into details here, but Group Treasurers should be aware that Groups share the privilege of the Boy Scouts Association in being regarded as educational charities, and exempt from Income Tax in respect of any income of theirs, including the annual value of Group headquarters owned by them. If they pay a rent for their headquarters which is less than the annual value, they are entitled to deduct the tax on the rent when they pay the next instalment, and they must of course pay the tax they have deducted to the Inland Revenue, but they can obtain exemption from tax in respect of the excess of the annual value over the rent.

It is wise to make friends with a practising accountant in the neighbourhood and get advice from him.

Insurance

The Group Committee's duty is to see that the Group is fully covered by insurance, for Scouters, boys and property.

Insurance on buildings, equipment and boats is dealt with on pages 94-96, but there are other risks to be covered, and they can be mentioned now.

Scouters' Indemnity Insurance. Accidents will happen, and Scouters may find themselves confronted with claims, sometimes for very large sums, for legal liability arising out of accidents that occur during organised *Scout* work. I.H.Q. has taken out a policy which covers all Scouters in the United Kingdom, and pays the premiums, so that G.S.M.s and Group Committees may rest easy on that score.

Personal Accident and Medical Expenses Insurance. Every Group should be insured against accidents and medical expenses incurred in connection with them. There is no compulsion to join the policy taken out by I.H.Q., but I strongly recommend doing so, as it provides better and cheaper cover than is normally obtainable elsewhere.

Some Counties and Districts insure all their Groups, and recover the premiums from the Groups. The G.S.M. who has not so far been concerned with this business should therefore enquire what the District arrangements are, and if his Group is not covered, he should arrange with his Treasurer to get it covered as soon as possible. The present rate is as low as 2d. a boy, and the policy covers such items as medical or other expenses arising out of accidents during actual *Scout* work, authorised or controlled by the Scouters concerned, £100 at death, £500 for total loss of two limbs, travelling or personal expenses incurred in the return home of a boy who has had an accident or been taken ill at camp, and certain disablement benefits. Extensions can be obtained for travel abroad, air travel, flights in the course of air training, and for activities such as building work and money-raising events, which are outside the terms of the ordinary policy.

Leaflets regarding this policy can be obtained from I.H.Q. and should be carefully studied.

The greatest care should be taken when a claim arises, and a notification must be sent to I.H.Q. *at once,* when the insurance policy is one taken out through them. It is imperative that no liability must ever be admitted or implied by anyone connected with the Group, and the existence of a policy should never be disclosed to anyone who may have an interest in making charges which may form part of a claim. The insurance brokers negotiate a settlement with the claimant, and this may be endangered if these rules are not strictly adhered to, especially when legal liability is in question.

CHAPTER 8

HEADQUARTERS AND EQUIPMENT

MOST Groups obtain accommodation in Church premises, schools or village halls, and share it with others. Although many Groups have reason to be grateful for such facilities, such an arrangement is often unsatisfactory, and makes good *Scout* programmes very difficult. There is often no security of tenure, and the Group may be turned out at the whim of the owner. The Troop may arrive for their weekly meeting and find that the room is being used for something else. Patrol and Six corners cannot be established, for no decorations can be hung upon the walls, and equipment cannot be stored.

At the same time, the use of Church or school premises by sponsored Groups may be the best means of keeping close contact with the Sponsoring Authority and of being recognised as an integral part of the work of the Church or school.

At least, in such cases, every endeavour should be made to get the exclusive use of a room where gear can be stored and small meetings such as the Court of Honour can be held. However small and humble, such a place is " home " to the Group. Perhaps also a locked cupboard can be placed somewhere in the premises where the main meetings are held, and used for the miscellaneous gear which is required for Pack and Troop meetings. It is a great trial to have to carry such stuff to and from home for each meeting, and the things most urgently needed are just the things that have been left behind.

However difficult it may be in such surroundings, an effort must be made to provide some *Scout* " atmosphere " for meetings. Folding screens for Patrols and Sixes, and portable decorations, are often contrived and make a wonderful difference. If there are hooks in the walls, or permission can be obtained to put them in, the Patrols can bring their own treasures out and hang them in their corners.

Even if the sections can only have the use of such premises once a week, there is no reason why the Patrols in the Boy Scout and Senior Scout Troops should not find dens of their own. This is a real challenge to the drive and ingenuity of Patrol Leaders. Dens have been discovered in all sorts of places—an attic in a parent's house, part of a garage, even a disused chicken-house—and although a hygiene expert might frown upon it, the boys are immensely pleased with it and spend hours decorating it. Patrol spirit and the leadership of the Patrol Leader leap ahead when the Patrol has found a home of its own, where even the Scoutmaster cannot enter without asking permission.

It is the duty of the G.S.M. to obtain the use of suitable accommodation for the Group (P.O.R. 172(2)) and of the Group Committee to help him to do so (P.O.R. 202(i)). It should be the ambition of every Group to have "a place of its own," even if it takes twenty years to realise the ambition. Some Groups have taken longer than that, but have succeeded at last.

If the Group consists of three or four sections, meeting twice a week, and has in addition Patrol meetings, instruction classes, and the numerous other meetings which a live Group needs, there is plenty to keep a headquarters of one's own fully occupied. Perhaps also it may be shared by a Girl Guide Company which will make its contribution to the expense. With a careful sharing of duties between the Scouters, the headquarters can be open every night in the week. It is particularly desirable that the Senior Scouts and Rovers, who are often busy with evening classes and study many nights in the week, should have dens of their own into which they can drop, when they have some spare moments, and meet their friends.

Clearly, plans for acquiring a place of one's own need to be very carefully laid. They need not be confined to putting up a new building. Some very successful Group headquarters have been set up in adapted private houses, of the kind that are not readily let as residences. Separate rooms can be provided for Scouters, a Cub lair, Patrol dens and rooms for Seniors and Rovers. Perhaps there is a good-sized garden at the back which can also be used for fire-lighting and other outdoor tests. A hall can even be built there as funds are available, but that is not always a necessity. There is usually a school hall round the corner which can be used for main meetings.

But whether you build or adapt, quite large funds will be necessary, and the Group Committee should set up a separate Headquarters Fund, into which subscriptions and the proceeds of many a money-raising effort can be paid. Until there is a reasonable sum in that special fund, plans cannot be translated into action. It is well to give a warning at this point. Cases are known where a Group Committee has concentrated so exclusively on its building fund that the present generation of boys has been starved of necessary equipment. That danger must be avoided. It is a good plan to divide the proceeds of money-raising efforts into two parts, and to pay the larger part (say, 75 per cent) into the building fund, while the smaller part (say, 25 per cent) is paid into the ordinary Group funds.

If it is decided to put up a new building, the first thing is to find a piece of land, and that is no easy matter in a built-up area. But even there, waste pieces of land of awkward shape may be discovered, and the Group Committee can enlist the help of friendly estate agents, or the Surveyor of the local authority, in the search for such plots. It is no use just getting permission to put up a building on someone else's land; security is essential, and it is almost always necessary to buy the freehold. Certainly nothing less than a 99 years' leasehold should be considered.

Throughout the planning, the advice of experts will be needed, and the G.S.M. will be wise to include a number of them in the Group Committee. At one stage or another, you will need a surveyor, an architect, a builder, a plumber, an electrician. Some of them may well be discovered in the ranks of the boys' parents, or among the Old Scouts. If there are too many of them to elect to the Group Committee, the alternative is to form a special Building sub-Committee, consisting of the experts, plus the G.S.M., the Treasurer and one or two Group Committee members.

It is essential to secure expert advice when land is being bought, in order to comply with all legal requirements (see also page 90).

This is not a technical handbook on building, and I will confine myself to one or two special points which affect Group headquarters. The greatest care must be taken to see that the plans are drawn up so as to meet the standards laid down by the Local Authority in matters of sanitation, and indeed the kind of building which may be erected on a particular site. It is no use planning to build a wooden hut on a piece of land if the local regulations insist that the building must be brick or stone. We must be scrupulous about obtaining licences and permits, and keeping strictly within their terms, however unscrupulous we may hear that some of our neighbours are.

In making a building plan, it is well to design the headquarters so that when it is complete it will contain all that you need—main hall, dens, Cub lair, Scouters' room, kitchen, canteen, lavatories and storage space. But if the designer is clever, it can be built by instalments as funds are available. Do not wait several years for your complete headquarters if you can get part of it at once.

Plan, moreover, so that the boys and their supporters can do as much as possible themselves. If the Group has obtained the help of the necessary experts to supervise the whole thing, a quite surprising amount of the work can be done by the non-experts. Parents and Old Scouts will rally round, and the cost of building will be materially reduced.

Above all, let us avoid the ornate and the magnificent. I remember being reduced to awed silence at viewing a

Group headquarters, the interior of which was painted egg-shell blue, with a stained-glass window in an apse at one end. Ball games, I was told, were strictly forbidden, but that didn't matter as much as I might have thought, for the boys were only allowed inside the place once a week. The rest of the time it was let to pay the expense!

The decoration of the interior must show it is a Scout place, and should be done very largely by the boys themselves; including such useful things as knot-boards, progress charts, Scouting trophies and a large notice-board. I like to see pictures of the Founder and of the present Chief Scout, and I would make a special plea for a picture of Her Gracious Majesty, herself a Guide and so delightfully interested in our two Movements. Groups in other parts of the Commonwealth and Empire would not dream of being without such a picture.

Lastly, do not let your decorations be so permanent that they become dingy and out of date. It is good for each generation of Scouts to put up their own decorations, to their own taste.

I recommend reference to the I.H.Q. pamphlet, "Our own place."

Grants

In the last chapter, I pointed out that it is not against Scouting principles to accept grant-aid. In the erection of a Group headquarters it is entirely justifiable to ask for such help. Both the Ministry of Education and the Local Education Authority have wide powers to give financial help to voluntary organisations, under Sections 41 and 53 of the Education Act, 1944, and the Social and Physical Training Grant Regulations, 1939, respectively.

The procedure is by way of an application to the Local Education Authority, probably through the local Youth Committee. It must be supported by the District Commissioner, and if the Scouts have a representative on the Youth Committee, he should be properly briefed before the application is considered.

Many applications are prejudiced by being badly presented. It is essential that a complete scheme should be drawn up, and the prescribed forms fully and accurately completed. The Grants Department at I.H.Q. is very ready to help Groups in this respect, and I cannot too strongly recommend that Group Committees should seek their advice before submissions are made, and that the application forms, completed in pencil, should be sent there for examination.

It must be remembered, too, that no grant will be obtainable if the Group has begun work on a scheme before making the application.

If the Local Education Authority approves an application, it may either make a grant itself, or (more likely) it may forward it to the Ministry of Education. As the Ministry consults I.H.Q. before it comes to a decision, it is obvious wisdom for the Group Committee to have consulted I.H.Q. before sending the application in.

In view of the provisions of the Town and Country Planning Act, 1953, you may have to pay a higher price for your property than the price which it would fetch if it were still to be used for its present purpose (*e.g.* as agricultural land), but you should get expert advice in order to avoid paying an excessive price.

The Ministry is empowered to make a grant even when a price has to be paid above the existing use value, so long as the District Valuer certifies that the figure does not exceed the amount he is prepared to recommend to the Ministry for acceptance. Moreover, the Ministry is prepared to ask the District Valuer to negotiate purchase on behalf of the Group.

The local Planning Authority has to give permission for the type of building that may be erected on the land, and previous enquiry should be made at the Council Office in order to find out how to proceed.

It may be added that I.H.Q. also receives a small annual

grant from King George V Jubilee Trust to help with new headquarters or other schemes involving capital expenditure.

Upkeep of Headquarters

There is no excuse for dirt or slovenliness in a Scout headquarters. It is a bad example to the boys, for it is contrary to the Scout Law. And yet so many headquarters are bad advertisements for Scouting—the outside surroundings neglected and unkempt, the notice-board short of paint, windows broken, rubbish on the unswept floor, dirt in every corner. However humble our headquarters may be, let us at least see that they are clean and reasonably warm, that the windows open and shut, and minor repairs are promptly done.

The Group Council and the Court of Honour can do much to encourage pride of possession on the part of Scouters and *Scouts* alike.

Equipment

Every Group needs equipment, the most expensive part of which is camping gear, and a good deal of foresight is needed on the part of the G.S.M. and Group Council in estimating what needs to be bought or renewed. Beside the heavy Patrol tents and feeding shelters used for summer camps, light-weight stuff is required for Patrol week-end camping. Ideally, each Patrol should have a complete set of equipment for a week-end camp and be made entirely responsible for it, but where that is not yet possible, the Troop can hold one or two sets which Patrols can borrow in turns.

Separate training gear, such as ropes, balls and signalling flags, should be provided for Pack and Troop, or there will be endless wrangles as to who lost what.

It is hoped that the Scoutmaster will find someone to take charge of all the gear—a sensible and efficient Quartermaster, perhaps one of the A.S.M.s. It needs constant supervision, especially when camp gear is being put away for the winter. If it were the Quartermaster's job to instruct the Troop as to the repair of guy lines, the cleaning of dixies and the care of axes, there would be less caustic comments from Commissioners who visit camps. On the other hand, the Q.M. must avoid succumbing to the temptation of refusing to allow anyone to use anything in case it gets damaged.

All ordinary repairs should be done by the boys themselves, and they should be encouraged to make as much of their gear as they can.

Sea Scout Troops have additional expenses to meet in the way of boats. They are very expensive, and the Group Committee will have to plan well ahead so as to have the money available. There are special Sea Scout funds at I.H.Q. to help in obtaining boats and equipment, especially if the Troop is "Admiralty recognised."

Except in the case of new Groups, grants for equipment from public funds are rarely justified, but if the District Commissioner does approve of an application being made, the procedure is the same as indicated under "Grants" above, but any grant obtainable is usually from the Local Education Authority and not from the Ministry of Education. Some Authorities do not make cash grants for equipment, but keep a stock of equipment which can be obtained by a Group on permanent loan.

Security of ownership

So long as everything is going smoothly, legal questions about who owns the Group's property do not arise, and they tend to be overlooked. Not until the Group is being disbanded, or some dispute arises, does anybody bother about them, and then it is too late. Much equipment has been lost to the Scout Movement, after heated dispute, just because a Group could not prove its ownership.

I cannot urge too strongly that every Group should follow strictly the safe rule (P.O.R. 204): "It is most important that, where a Group possesses property of any value, such property should be vested in trustees under a Deed of Trust, of which a model form is obtainable without charge from I.H.Q." In these days, almost every Group possesses property of value, when we remember that the word "property" includes all the Group equipment. Advice about this is readily obtainable from the Legal Adviser at I.H.Q. Two or more Trustees will be needed, and the Group will have no difficulty in getting responsible local people to serve. It is wise to choose young ones, so that the trouble of changing trustees does not often arise.

One advantage of using the model Deed of Trust drawn up by I.H.Q. is that, if the Group is disbanded, the property passes to the Boy Scouts Association for the benefit of *Scouts* in that neighbourhood. If there is no such deed, the position may be very difficult in the event of disbandment. Quite often, the property remains in the hands of those who happen to hold it at the moment. P.O.R. cannot provide rules for the destination of such property, but the Local Association is recommended to take charge of it, with a view to using it for the benefit of any new Group that may be formed in the place, or if no such Group is formed within a reasonable time, for the benefit of other local Groups.

It sometimes happens that Trust Deeds cannot be found when they are wanted. Trustees have died or moved away, and changes of G.S.M. have resulted in the whole thing being overlooked. It is for the Group Committee to decide where the Trust Deed should be stored for safe keeping, and to keep a permanent note of its resting place, but I.H.Q. offers to take custody of Deeds of Trust on behalf of the Movement, and that is probably the best place for them

If the Group possesses property of certain types, it can

ask I.H.Q. if the Boy Scouts Association Trust Corporation will accept trusteeship. The Corporation is incorporated under the Companies Act, 1929, and is licensed by the Lord Chancellor as a trust corporation. This is a most valuable service to the Movement, for the Corporation is a permanent incorporated body, which does not die, and no change of trustees is ever required.

The Corporation can only accept trusteeship of the following classes of property:—

(*a*) freehold land, not subject to a mortgage, and free from any liabilities such as road-making charges or inconvenient restrictions on the use of the property;

(*b*) stocks and shares, provided that there is no liability attaching thereto;

(*c*) leaseholds in special cases only, where the rent is purely nominal, the property is not subject to any mortgage or other liability, and there are no covenants which may entail expenditure in respect of repairs, etc., or which contain inconvenient restrictions on the use of the property.

The Legal Adviser at I.H.Q. will send a Group full particulars on request. A small fee is payable for the services of the Corporation, but it is amply repaid in the course of time by the avoidance of all trouble and expense for the appointment of new trustees.

In the case of a sponsored Group, special care is needed to place on record what property belongs to the Sponsoring Authority and what to the Group. This is dealt with in the chapter on sponsored Groups (pages 119-120), but it may be remarked here that the Group still needs to execute a Deed of Trust for the property that belongs to it.

Insurance

No Group in these days can afford the risk of incurring a heavy, possibly crippling, loss caused by fire or burglary.

It is essential, therefore, that the Group Committee should see that its risks are fully covered by insurance. It should realise what those risks are, and how they can be covered most economically. They are free to place their insurances where they like, but the I.H.Q. policies mentioned below can be confidently recommended, for they have been drawn up after long experience to meet the special conditions of the Scout Movement.

The risks covered by the I.H.Q. policies which concern property or equipment are as shown below. Other insurances were dealt with on pages 83-84.

Property Owners' Risk. An extension of the Scoutmasters' Indemnity Policy (see page 83) can be arranged to cover the property owners' and premises risk for Groups which own or are responsible for the upkeep of premises or camping grounds.

Scout Property and Equipment Policy. This policy covers such risks as fire, lightning, or explosion damaging headquarters buildings and contents; fire, burglary, housebreaking, and many other risks for buildings and the whole of their contents; the same risks for camping equipment anywhere in Great Britain or in transit; for personal kit (other than Wolf Cub property) at camp or in transit; and for equipment on hire.

The policy resulted from long negotiations, and can be confidently recommended, both for the full risks covered and for the low premiums.

Sea Scout Insurance Policy. This policy aims at covering all risks incidental to the use of boats by Sea Scouts, apart from those which are already covered by the general Scout policies.

Full information regarding all these policies is obtainable from I.H.Q. The amounts insured should be reviewed, at least annually, to cover rises of price levels and additional gear.

Careful attention should be paid to the precautions which must be taken in the event of a claim (see page 84).

Inventory

For many reasons, Group Committees should ensure that careful inventories of property and equipment are prepared and kept up to date. Important additions should be recorded at once, and the whole inventory revised annually, preferably on the date to which the annual accounts are made up.

I would suggest that the Group Treasurer should undertake this job himself, with the help of the G.S.M., the section leaders and the Patrol Leaders for the equipment with which they are particularly concerned. I include the Patrol Leaders because it is good training for them in thrift and the careful use of equipment. Boys can be thoughtless and wasteful unless they know that they will be called to account.

The inventories are required for various purposes: —

(i) to be sent annually to the Local Association with a copy of the audited accounts (P.O.R. 206 and 211);

(ii) for use in connection with insurance policies;

(iii) for attachment to the Group's Deed of Trust.

I would again remind readers that when the inventory is revised, the approximate total value should be reckoned up, and any increase covered by additional insurance cover.

CHAPTER 9

RECORDS AND CORRESPONDENCE

THIS chapter may be more than usually dull, but it is a very necessary one, for letter-writing and the keeping of records are not the strongest points in our Scout organisation. It was not surprising in the old days, when the Scoutmaster ran his little Troop single-handed and did everything himself. There is little excuse for it now, when the Group is a family unit of several sections, interdependent upon one another.

As in most other matters, much depends upon the G.S.M. in the first instance to get a clear and simple system installed, and to keep an eye on it from time to time in order to see that things are kept up to date. Each Group will have its own way of keeping records, and I am far from wishing to urge any universal system. But for the benefit of the newcomer it may be well to list the main records which, in some form or another, every Group should keep. I omit here the accounts and inventories, which have been mentioned in Chapter 7.

Admission forms. These are often called " Parents' Consent forms," and are used to explain to the parents of the newly-joined boy what is involved in joining a Group. They contain a detachable part which the parent signs and returns to the section leader, consenting to the boy joining. Supplies of the I.H.Q. forms can be bought from the Scout Shops. They have the advantage of being nicely produced, and are worth considering. But many Groups prefer a home-made version of their own, and even if the official form is used, it needs an inset giving such local particulars as the address of the headquarters, the times of meetings and arrangements for buying uniform. A form by itself is a pretty cold welcome to a Pack or Troop, and needs to be supplemented by an early visit to the parents by the section leader or G.S.M., but it is worth obtaining the parent's consent in writing, and ensuring that the conditions of joining are understood. So many boys are brought along by their friends that the receipt of a form may be the first news the parent have about this great event in their son's life. But all the more reason for a Scouter to go and see them, quickly.

Record of boys' subscriptions. Simple, pocket-size booklets can be obtained at the Scout Shop for recording boys' weekly subscriptions. In the case of the Cub Pack, the record is kept by the Cubmaster or one of her assistants, and the weekly total of the subscriptions, when checked, is entered in her Petty Cash book.

In the Boy Scout and Senior Scout Troops, the record is part of the responsibility of the Patrol Leader, who hands the money collected to the Scoutmaster or one of his assistants designated for the job. It is only fair to the boy leader that the amount handed over should be checked at the time with the total shown in his book. The Scoutmaster will be wise to have a look at the Patrol books once a month or so, in order to ensure that the slack and irregular member of the Patrol—and what Patrol has not got one young gentleman like that?—gets chased for his arrears, and is not allowed to get away with it. It is a good thing if the books can be kept at the headquarters, so that the Second can get hold of his Patrol book if the Patrol Leader is unexpectedly absent.

Arrangements for the collection of subscriptions from members of the Rover Crew are apt to be elastic, if any exist at all, but the Rover Mate is the person to collect them when he sees the Rovers. A monthly, rather than a weekly, rate of subscription may well be more satisfactory.

Personal records. These records of the boys, and of their progress, are a vital part of the Group's work. They are often kept on cards, which can easily be moved round in a box if the boy changes his Six or Patrol, and can be sent up with him when he moves from Pack to Troop. However the records are kept, it really is important that the Scoutmaster, for example, should have access to the record of every Cub that comes up into the Troop. Again, when a Scout moves away and is transferred to a Troop at his new home, his new Scoutmaster will be delighted (even if surprised) to get the boy's record from his old Group.

The particulars required for each boy are normally as follows: full name and address, date of joining, date invested, religious denomination, date of birth, Six or Patrol, tests passed (with dates), badge record, promotions (to Second or Sixer, to Second or Patrol Leader), date of going up to the next section or of transfer to another Group, or sadly, the date of leaving *and why*. This "why" must be recorded as faithfully as we know how, and we may learn a lot by gathering together the cards of boys who left during the year and studying the reasons why they left. Were they just experimenters who found Scouting was not what they wanted? Or was it our fault that they left—because they failed to make the progress they expected, or because the programmes were dull and routine?

Either on the card itself, or perhaps preferably in a little private notebook, the Cubmaster or Scoutmaster will find it useful to keep personal notes about each boy. Not, if you please, a catalogue of his failings, added to whenever he displeases you, but notes of his strengths as well as his weaknesses. By using his strong points you can often help him to overcome his weak ones.

I must leave it to the G.S.M. to decide whether he needs a duplicate of these personal records in his own possession. I rather hope he will not, for it is a frightful nuisance to make sure that they are kept up to date, unless both the G.S.M. and the section leaders are very businesslike. But it is part of the G.S.M.'s supervision to look at the section leader's records from time to time, not only to see that they are kept written up, but to learn from them how each boy is getting on—and especially which boys are not getting on.

It is valuable to prepare a large progress chart for each Six and Patrol, to be hung up in the headquarters, on which are recorded all the tests passed by each boy in his progress from Tenderpad to Leaping Wolf, and from Tenderfoot to First Class and beyond. Here is a chance for the Group artist or draughtsman, but they can be obtained more prosaically from the Scout Shops.

Proficiency Badge certificate books. I.H.Q. sell these books in three varieties—for Wolf Cub badges, for " under 15 " Scout badges, and for " over 15 " Scout badges. Section leaders will be well advised to buy these through their local Badge Secretaries, so that when a boy goes to be examined by the Badge Examiner he can take a blank certificate with him and get it signed on the spot if he passes.

Log Books. As a record of the history of the Pack or Troop or Crew, a log book is of great value. No one who has organised a reunion of Old Scouts, and watched the enthusiasm with which they have examined the old log books, and recognised themselves and their friends as they were years ago, needs convincing about this. But we are busy with all sorts of other things, and tend to put off starting one, or fail to keep it up to date if we have one.

But even if we have failed in the past, let us resolve to make a new start. Let the boys do as much as possible, and put in charge one of your assistants who is prepared to work on it. Here is the chance for your artists and photographers, for the pictorial record is more valuable than the written word. We are storing up a mass of entertaining reminiscences for ourselves and the boys for the years that lie ahead.

Court of Honour Minute Book.

Group Council Minute Book.

Group Committee Minute Book.

These explain themselves, I hope.

Address Book. For the addresses and telephone numbers of the people the G.S.M. needs to be in touch with, especially the District Commissioner and his A.D.C.s, the Local Association Secretary, Treasurer and Badge Secretary, the L.A. Badge Examiners, other local G.S.M.s and Scouters, the members of the Group Committee and of the experts he can call upon, the Local Education Authority Youth Officer, and so on.

List of books that are Group property. Libraries are dealt with in the miscellaneous chapter at the end, but even if you don't go in for anything so ambitious, you *must* have some books which are Group property, for example some of the technical Scout books which it is unreasonable to expect Scouters to buy for themselves. We need to keep a list of them, perhaps on the shelf in headquarters where the books are kept, and to provide space for recording by whom they have been borrowed.

File of pamphlets. I.H.Q. publish a range of useful pamphlets, many of which should be in the possession of every Group. A list of some of them appears in Appendix A. Here again, a note should be made in the file whenever one is borrowed and taken away from headquarters by one of the Scouters.

File of L.A. Circulars. "I know I saw one of those circulars the D.C. sent round about so-and-so, but where is it?" It should be in the file at headquarters, if there is a file.

"*Policy, Organisation and Rules.*" Certainly at least one copy on the headquarters shelf, kept up to date by reference to the Headquarters Notices in "The Scouter."

"*The Scouter.*" Although it is to be hoped that each of the Scouters has his own copy at home, it is a good thing to keep a file of issues at headquarters for reference there.

Census forms. The figures compiled at the annual census at 31st March deserve more attention than they often get at Group level, and copies of the figures for the current year and several past years should be kept together in a file. It is one of the tasks of the Group Council to consider these figures each year, and much can be learned from a study of the details, as compared not only with last year but also with several previous years. It is a convenient way of ascertaining whether the sections of the Group are making progress, or the reverse. If, for example, the number of boys in the Troop remains small, although there are plenty of boys about, why is it and what shall we do about it? If the number of Second Class Scouts is too small, what can we do to encourage more progress up the Scout ladder?

As the Local Association Secretary has to make a summary for the whole area, and send it on to the County Secretary, who makes a County summary for I.H.Q., it is obvious that one Group which fails to complete its form properly is holding up the whole process. So let us complete the forms just before the closing date rather than after, and then remember to post them.

As the census form is also the application for re-registration of the Group, it follows that a Group which fails to send in its figures altogether gets struck off the roll. It serves them right, for they will have had several reminders, but it means that one fine day, when the Scoutmaster wants some Tenderfoot badges, he discovers the Badge Secretary will not supply him, for his Group has no official existence. The process of registering the Group has then to be carried through all over again—but what a waste of everyone's time!

Correspondence file. Important business letters need to be kept, with a note of the answer sent or a carbon copy of the reply. Provided, that is, that a reply was sent. It has been a reproach too often in the past that Scouters do not answer letters, and lots of jokes have been made about it. But they are not very funny jokes, for failure to reply to letters which need an answer is a breach of the Scout law of courtesy. Let us see that no Scouter in our Group is guilty of such a breach.

It is an even worse reproach that some Scouters write rude letters. No one can teach his boys to be courteous if he behaves rudely himself. We all get irritated at times, and we may be sorely provoked, but that does not absolve us from being courteous. And, incidentally, how much more effective is the retort courteous than a stream of invective, or a display of our gift of sarcasm!

While I am on the subject of correspondence, I can mention certain rules by which we are expected to be guided in our Groups. You will find them in P.O.R. 48-53. It is certainly " the desire of I.H.Q. that correspondence shall be reduced as much as possible." Contrary to general belief, I.H.Q. originates very little correspondence. I should guess than 90 per cent of the letters written by members of I.H.Q. are in reply to letters which have arrived from outside.

In general, letters designed for I.H.Q. should be sent through the District and County Commissioners, but there are certain exceptions: —

(*a*) matters of extreme urgency, such as an enquiry about a doubtful character where there is not time to go through the normal channels (see page 42);

(*b*) cases of accident involving possible insurance claims;

(*c*) orders for the Scout Shops;

(*d*) requests for stock forms, except that for cheap rail fares, which are supplied to Local Association Secretaries only;

(*e*) enquiries regarding the training of Scouters and applications for forms to attend training courses at Gilwell Park, which can be sent direct to the Camp Chief at that address.

Lastly, there are two rules which for the sake of discipline and good order must be strictly observed: —

(i) "Correspondence relating to *Scout* matters must not be addressed to any Royal Personage, to any Department of State, or to any Embassy or Legation at home or abroad, except through I.H.Q." (P.O.R. 52). No, you must not write direct to Her Majesty and ask her to open your Group Bazaar!

(ii) "No member of the Association may express opinions in the public Press on any matter of *Scout* policy or principle or be concerned in any sound or television broadcast referring or relating to the Scout Movement without the previous approval of I.H.Q." (P.O.R. 53). The G.S.M. should warn his Scouters not to rush into print in the Movement's defence, if the local paper publishes something to which they take exception. Again, everyone will be delighted if the B.B.C. wants to televise your Group show, BUT IT'S GOT TO BE GOOD.

CHAPTER 10

DUTY TO GOD IN THE GROUP

"ON my honour I promise that I will do my best—to do my duty to God . . ." Make no mistake about it, God comes first in the Scout Promise, and has always done so from the start of the Movement. It is clear, then, that the Scouters of a Group, who have themselves taken that Promise, must see that " Duty to God " comes first in their own lives and in all their thinking and planning. It must not be pushed into the background, or dealt with in a kind of watertight compartment.

The subject is very fully dealt with in a pamphlet, "Scouting, Religion and the Churches," published by I.H.Q. A copy was sent to every Group in 1954. I would strongly recommend that personal copies should be in the hands of all the section leaders, and that G.S.M.s should arrange to discuss some part of the subject at meetings of the Group Council. It is so easy to take it for granted. The special value of the pamphlet is that it has been agreed by all the members of the Religious Advisory Panel at I.H.Q., and they represent all the principal religious denominations in this country.

I cannot do more in this book than draw attention to a few points. Most of what I shall say relates equally to open and to sponsored Groups, but a number of matters which specially affect the latter will be dealt with in the next chapter.

In open Groups, the example of the Scouters and the atmosphere of the Group mean almost everything, for many of the boys—perhaps the majority—may not be attached to any place of worship, may get little or no encouragement at home, and may reach their first dim understanding of God from their Troop or Pack. Where the Scouters are themselves regular Church members, all will be well, but that is frequently not the case. We know that the Churches do not produce enough leaders for their own Groups, let alone open Groups also, and we must do our best with the leaders we have. But at least we must be sure that we do not give warrants to atheists or convinced agnostics. At least we must expect a Scouter who has no settled convictions to be seriously seeking, and not just leaving the whole thing to some later date which may never come. To be a " seeker " is the next best thing to being a " finder." I am sure that our Scouters have the best of intentions, and would not willingly let their boys down by word or deed.

For those who are seeking, I would strongly recommend John Thurman's book, " God and the Open Scout Group," for it was written specially for them. Moreover, short courses on the Law and Promise, and on " Duty to God," are organised in many places to help such people. Most Counties have a small staff of County Chaplains of various denominations, from whom the G.S.M. can get advice.

The Religious Policy

The religious policy of the Movement is contained in P.O.R. 10-12, and was agreed by B.-P. right at the beginning with the heads of the Churches. This was a most important step, which has ensured us the support of responsible Church authorities ever since. It is binding on all who serve the Scout Movement. We shall consider now those parts of it which affect Groups which are not composed of boys of one denomination.

In the first place, we must be punctilious to see that *Scouts* who are attached to a Church are encouraged by the Group to fulfil their duties to it, and that no Group arrangements will interfere with their doing so, or give rise to a clash of loyalties. In one respect, the G.S.M. of an open Group needs to be more knowledgeable in matters of religion than his next-door neighbour in a Church Group, for he will have in the Group *Scouts* who are attached to several different denominations, and who have different forms of obligation to their Churches. It is very desirable, therefore, that he should be in friendly contact with the incumbents and ministers of the Churches from which his boys come, and reach agreement with them as to what the Group can and cannot do. To help him further, I.H.Q. publishes a little pamphlet, "The Religious Obligations of Scouts," which contains statements from each of the principal Churches as to what is expected of their boys. Every section leader of an open Group should have a copy of this.

The Scouters must not take up a negative attitude to this; they must give active encouragement to their boys, who are apt to make every kind of excuse to dodge their Church duties. Hence P.O.R. 10(3) says: "Where a Group consists of *Scouts* of various religions they should be encouraged to attend the services of their own denominations, and Group Church parades should not be held. In camp, any form of daily prayer and of weekly divine service should be of the simplest character, attendance being voluntary."

It is obviously not playing the game to arrange a Church parade at the parish church and expect a Roman Catholic or a Jew to attend. It is also undesirable to arrange church parades in rotation at churches of different denominations, for we must respect the convictions of others, and P.O.R. 10(4) says: "Where it is not permissible under the rules of the religion of any *Scout* to attend religious observances other than those of his own Church, the Scouters of the Group must see that such rules are strictly observed while the *Scout* is under their control."

On the other hand, it is an excellent practice to have a Group tradition that on (say) the first Sunday in the month each *Scout* attends his own Church in uniform, and that unattached *Scouts* should, with their parents' permission, go with one of the Scouters to his Church. Sometimes, the Group comes together at its headquarters after the services for a Going-up Ceremony, or some such function, when the Pack can see the Troop and vice versa.

District Church parades are under the control of the District Commissioner (P.O.R. 11) and will probably be confined to a special occasion such as St. George's Day. Many clergy have no objection to their boys attending such a special service, but the rule is careful to say that " under no circumstances should a G.S.M. urge *Scouts* to attend places of worship other than those of his own denomination."

With the co-operation of the Churches, membership of a Group and all that it involves can often be a bridge over which a boy can cross to membership of a Church. The hope that this might be so was in B.-P.'s mind when he drafted the first sub-paragraph of the religious policy, for P.O.R. 10 (1) says: " It is expected that every *Scout* shall belong to some religious denomination and attend its services." It is the same kind of language as is used in the *Scout* Law—"A Scout's honour is to be trusted," and so on. We must do our best to see that our boys live up to that expectation. The sure fact that in these days it is difficult is no excuse for shirking it, but much depends upon the encouragement a boy gets from his parents, and it is one of the things which the G.S.M. or section leader must discuss with the parents when their boy applies to join the Group. Usually, parents who go nowhere to church will say, " He can do what he likes," and much will then depend upon whether the Scouter goes to Church himself. The Scouter must also bear in mind that under P.O.R. 10 (5) it is his duty, in the case of a boy who is not attached to any Church, to ask the parents' permission to put him in touch with the Church to which his parents belong or in which he was baptised. The time when their son is being asked to take the *Scout* Promise is often an opportunity for a clergyman to call upon the parents, and perhaps persuade them to let their boy come back to Church, or, better still, to resume membership themselves. We can at least let the clergyman have the opportunity—if he fails, we have done our best, and it may be that another chance will present itself as the boy's understanding of the meaning of the Promise becomes clearer.

The Law and Promise

Whether in an open or a sponsored Group, denominational religious teaching is a matter for the clergy, although Scouters who are themselves instructed Church members can do much to help.

The Scouters' great contribution comes through their teaching of the Scout Law and Promise. These are the foundations of the Brotherhood of Scouts, and no boy is a *Scout*, and no adult is a Scouter, until the Promise has been taken. Methods and practices in Scouting vary considerably from country to country, according to national customs and climate, but the Promise is universal.

It must be the task of the G.S.M. and the Group Council to give constant thought to the teaching of the Law and Promise, for on this depends the tone of every section of the Group. It is to be feared that in some Groups this takes place when a boy is being invested, and is then dropped out of sight. Cases have been known where a Queen's Scout shows no deeper understanding of the Law and Promise than he did when a Tenderfoot. It should be the invariable custom in every good Group that no boy should be allowed to take the next step forward (*e.g*. from 1st Star to 2nd Star Cub, or from 2nd Class to 1st Class Scout) until the section leader is satisfied that he has made a corresponding advance in his understanding and practice of the Law and Promise. The whole Movement needs to pay far more attention to this vital matter, and it is for G.S.M.s to give the lead to the Group Council and exercise constant supervision.

The ideals of Scouting have many enemies in these days, who challenge our standards and our beliefs—atheists, agnostics, Communists. Attention has been drawn to this in a pamphlet issued jointly by the Boy Scouts and Girl Guides Associations—"A Challenge to Scouting—the Menace of Communism." This is dealt with further on pages 216-217.

On the next three sections on Prayers, Yarns and Stories, and Scouts' Owns, I recommend study of John Thurman's book, "God and the Open Scout Group," and, for Cub Scouters, Mrs. Addis's "Duty to God in the Wolf Cub Pack."

Prayers

Every *Scout* meeting should include a short period for prayers; the end of the meeting is usually the best time. Every day in camp should open and close with prayers. In an open Group, Roman Catholics and others who are not permitted to join in prayers with those of other Churches should withdraw. If there are several of them, the senior member should take prayers with them.

It still needs to be said that the period for prayers needs as careful preparation as the other parts of the programme, in order to ensure that they are short, simple and suitable, and that special occasions are not overlooked, such as the sickness of a *Scout,* or a Senior Scout's departure for National Service. The I.H.Q. publication, "Prayers for use in the Brotherhood of Scouts," provides a wide selection of prayers, but the Scouter may still need to find or compose a prayer for a special occasion.

Yarns and Stories

It is now generally recognised that a Cub Pack meeting is not complete without a story, but it is to be feared that Troop Scouters greatly neglect the value of the yarn. They are shy about it, and dubious of their abilities. But practice and sincerity are valuable allies, and there can be no doubt of the value of yarns in teaching the Law and Promise.

A boy finds difficulty in grasping an abstract idea, such as courtesy, but can understand it in terms of giving up his seat in a bus.

There is no lack of material for yarns if you look for them. Stories from the Bible itself (which boys will listen to when their Scouter tells them, though they may have shut their ears to them when they heard them in school), lives of great men, such as Grenfell of Labrador or Wilson of the Antarctic, lives of the more active Saints, anecdotes you find in your newspaper or magazine—these are just a few of the sources from which you can draw your material.

The Scouts' Own

Scouts' Owns are explained in P.O.R. 12 as being "gatherings of *Scouts* . . . held for the worship of God and to promote fuller realisation of the *Scout* Law and Promise," but they are supplementary to, and not in substitution for, the religious observances referred to in Rule 10. They have been well described as "something extra which a *Scout* does because he is a *Scout*."

There is much to be said for the regular holding of a *Scouts'* Own (and that means Cubs' Own, too) even in a sponsored Group, but the case is much stronger in the open Group, for a Scouts' Own may be the boys' first real experience of worship. Especially in camp, in beautiful open-air surroundings, a simple sincerity of worship of God comes naturally to a boy, and who can tell what such experiences may mean to him in later years? We do too little to encourage boys' sense of wonder at the marvels of God in nature.

Many Scouters, I know, feel doubtful of their ability to run a good Scouts' Own, but I can assure them that practice, and careful preparation, can overcome most of the difficulties, especially as the Patrol Leaders will be ready to take their full part, and there is plenty of help available in published literature. " Prayers for use in the Brotherhood of Scouts " has already been referred to; there is a " Scout Hymn Book," and, above all, there is invaluable help in a book called " Scouts' Owns," by Pat Leonard (now Bishop of Thetford); all are available at the Scout Shops.

Week-end camps

The G.S.M.'s part in relation to the general camping activities of the Group will be dealt with in Chapter 13, but one or two points should be mentioned here, as they affect " Duty to God " in an open Group.

It is undesirable that boys should be given opportunities of camping every week-end during the summer. They should not be taken away from their families week-end after week-end, nor should boys attached to Churches be kept away from the family of their Church. If Patrols go in rotation, every boy will get several week-ends during the season.

The clergy are usually very reasonable about letting their boys off, if they are consulted in advance and if they are not asked too frequently. In any case, it should be a condition for a boy to attend a camp that he should have got leave of absence from his choirmaster or Sunday School teacher, if he is involved in such activities.

Even at week-end camps, and on hikes and cycle tours, there should be an opportunity for a boy to attend Church, and, as mentioned above, the possibility of a Scouts' Own should be considered.

Lastly, a week-end camp should never be an excuse for an idle round of lounging, eating and sleeping. We cannot blame the clergy for objecting to camps of that kind, and we must see that part of the time is well occupied with a training programme.

CHAPTER 11

THE SPONSORED GROUP

IN Chapter 2 I mentioned sponsored Groups briefly, when writing of the registration of a Group. Now it is time to discuss them at greater length, and it may be well to repeat the points which were mentioned previously.

A Group is described as " sponsored " if it is connected with one of the sponsoring bodies listed in P.O.R. 179 (i). These bodies fall into five main categories: —

(i) Churches, and certain organisations allied thereto, including the Salvation Army, Y.M.C.A., Society of St. Vincent de Paul in England, Church Army, Church of England Temperance Society and Regnal League.

(ii) Universities, colleges and schools.

(iii) Hospitals and institutions.

(iv) Works.

(v) Special bodies such as the British Legion, National Association of Boys' Clubs, National Juvenile Templars Council, and others which may be approved by I.H.Q.

The Sponsoring Authority, who will be mentioned so frequently in this chapter, is the person appointed by the sponsoring body to carry out its functions. For simplicity we will call the Sponsoring Authority " he " and " him," although " he " is sometimes a Committee and not an individual.

About half the Groups in this country are sponsored, mostly by a church or school, and the other half are open. Sponsored Groups therefore constitute an extremely important element in the Movement here, and it is well worth taking trouble to see that the relationships between Scouting and the Sponsoring Authority are on the right

H

basis from the start. It is wise to bring the District Commissioner into consultation before any public steps are taken to form a sponsored Group, for it is he and the Local Association who approve its foundation. As usual, the main point to be considered is the local boys, and while there is usually plenty of room in towns for the two kinds of Groups, it is better to have an open Group in a village which is not large enough to support more than one, lest any boy who wants to be a *Scout* should be prevented from joining.

The I.H.Q. pamphlet, " The Sponsored Group," sets out the nature of a sponsored Group, the duties and responsibilities of the Sponsoring Authority and the G.S.M., and a number of special points that need to be considered. A new Sponsoring Authority should always be supplied with a copy, and be asked to consider the points in it with the D.C. or G.S.M., in order that he may understand our arrangements, and that his help and sympathy may be enlisted from the start. It is no use setting up a sponsored Group if the Sponsoring Authority is not in sympathy with it.

The registration of such a Group follows the same lines as described in Chapter 2, except that the Sponsoring Authority not only signs the form but also signs an undertaking to give the Group his support and encouragement.

The Sponsoring Authority

The person or Committee called by this name varies according to the type of sponsoring body. The Sponsoring Authority in the case of a Church of England Group, for example, must be " the incumbent or some individual appointed by him for the purpose " (P.O.R. 179 (iii)); in a school Group, he would be the headmaster; in a hospital Group, the Committee, or Medical Superintendent, or Matron, according to circumstances.

Once upon a time, sponsored Groups were known as " controlled Groups," and it was not surprising that some

"Controlling Authorities," as they were called, regarded the functions of control as far more important than showing a friendly interest in the affairs of the Group. The present expression "sponsored" conveys a better idea of the true function of the Sponsoring Authority. He is in friendly partnership with the G.S.M. and other Scouters. But he is neither sole partner nor sleeping partner in the firm. For this reason, Rule 179A was added to P.O.R. when the idea of control gave way to that of sponsorship. This lays upon the Sponsoring Authority certain definite responsibilities. He must—

"(1) accept the aims, methods and policy of the Association as set out in 'Scouting for Boys' and P.O.R., and the duty of endeavouring to ensure the continuity of the Group and the annual renewal of its registration;

"(2) agree to observe in particular the conditions of Rule 180 (of which more below);

"(3) record with the L.A. an agreement in regard to property in accordance with Rule 205;

"(4) undertake to give the G.S.M. the fullest possible assistance in carrying out the duties imposed upon him by Rule 182."

While the Sponsoring Authority accepts these duties, it is the corresponding duty of the Scouters of the Group to play fair and see that his rights are respected. They must be loyal to him and to the body he represents, whether it is a Church, a school or a hospital. Scouting has no use for the Scouters who use the premises and other facilities provided by the sponsoring body and do nothing in return.

The rights of the Sponsoring Authority are found in P.O.R. 180 and concern (i) the boys who may be admitted to the Group, (ii) the nomination of the Scouters, (iii) his right to be heard by the L.A. and the D.C. in certain circumstances, and (iv) his responsibility for religious training in certain cases. Some of these can be dealt with when we come to consider particular types of Groups.

Nomination of Scouters

The nomination of Scouters is an important right of the Sponsoring Authority, for no one can be appointed whom he does not want or who is not in sympathy with his work. But the right is one of nomination, not of appointment. It remains the duty of the D.C. and L.A. to satisfy themselves that the applicant is suitable to be a Scouter.

It was at one time very usual for a Sponsoring Authority to suggest himself as G.S.M., sometimes only for the purpose of greater control, and without any serious idea of carrying out the full duties. This is not a good plan, and P.O.R. 169 (v) now suggests that " except in special circumstances it is not desirable that the Sponsoring Authority should himself be appointed as, or carry out the duties of, G.S.M., unless the L.A. and D.C. are satisfied that he has time to carry out the complete duties of a G.S.M. as set out in Rule 173." The complete duties of a G.S.M. are, as we have seen, numerous and complex, and cannot normally be carried out by such a Sponsoring Authority as a busy parish priest. But to that rule there are, I am glad to say, some excellent exceptions.

Change of Sponsoring Authority

A change of Sponsoring Authority, such as the appointment of a new incumbent or headmaster, demands careful attention. The new man may know little or nothing of Scouting and have little idea of his duties in connection with the sponsored Group that he finds installed. It is the G.S.M.'s job to make friends with him as soon as he is settled in, and give him all the information he wants to have. He should receive a copy of the " Sponsored Group " pamphlet, and it may well be wise to ask him to sign the same undertaking as was given by his predecessor when the Group was registered. The wording can be obtained from form C, which the L.A. Secretary can supply. In difficult cases, the District Commissioner should be brought in, and especially where it seems possible that the Group may need to have its registration changed from sponsored to open.

Sponsoring Authority's right to be heard

P.O.R. 180 (3) gives a whole catalogue of circumstances in which the Sponsoring Authority has the right to be heard by the L.A. and D.C. We may be thankful that the right is rarely exercised, for the situation is usually delicate and far better dealt with by friendly and private conversations, which should be undertaken as early as possible. The G.S.M. should be in close touch with the D.C. in all such cases, and the help of the appropriate County Chaplain may be invoked by the D.C. through the County Commissioner in the case of a Church-sponsored Group.

There is one rule, tucked away under " Warrants," which is not widely known. Under P.O.R. 77 (ii), the L.A. and D.C. must give effect to the views of the Sponsoring Authority of a Church Group if he is dissatisfied with a Scouter of the Group solely on the ground that the Scouter is not fulfilling his religious duties either by his example or precept. The Sponsoring Authority is fully protected if one of the Scouters lets him down on religious grounds, but he is not entitled to demand his dismissal on any other grounds, such as moral character or technical efficiency. Such questions must be dealt with in the ordinary way by the D.C. and L.A.

The Group Committee

A Group Committee is as much required in a sponsored Group as in an open one, for equipment and finance are universal needs, and what has been said in Chapter 8 applies to both alike. But there are one or two ways in which the Group Committee can be of particular importance to a sponsored Group. It can be most valuable in preserving continuity where there is a change of Sponsoring Authority. The new man may know little or nothing of the Scout Movement and its methods. He may even be unsympathetic. A well-established Group Committee, consisting of respected members of the Church or school, can be most helpful in securing the confidence and friendliness of the new Sponsoring Authority.

It can also establish friendly relations with the other members of the Church or school, and secure the recognition of the Scout Group as a recognised part of the community. But this can only happen when the members of the Committee are themselves loyal members of that community. For that reason, it is always wise for the G.S.M. to ask the Sponsoring Authority to nominate some members of the Group Committee, and to approve the whole list of members.

Headquarters and Equipment

It is the duty of the Sponsoring Authority to help the G.S.M. to carry out his duties (P.O.R. 179A (4)), and one of those duties is to " help the Group to obtain suitable headquarters and the necessary equipment and opportunities for training " (P.O.R. 182 (5)). Difficulties of accommodation compel most sponsored Groups to share the use of rooms with other people, but we can look to the Sponsoring Authority to ensure that the Group has the regular use of whatever accommodation is available, and that the Pack or Troop is not thrown out whenever anything else turns up. On the Scout side, it is only right to offer to pay at least the cost of lighting, heating and cleaning, and to see that the room is left neat and tidy after meetings. Even so, the Group may be under considerable difficulties in not being able to put up its own decorations, and in being compelled to an unnatural silence owing to the proximity of another meeting in an adjoining room. We may have to make the best of these conditions, but it is not easy, and the G.S.M. should be able to rely upon the sympathetic help of the Sponsoring Authority in making the conditions as tolerable as possible.

It is for these reasons that the policy of the Movement

has always been that every Group should aim at possessing its own headquarters. In the case of a sponsored Group, this problem needs approaching with great care. There is a fear on the part of some Sponsoring Authorities that a Group which does not meet on their premises may loosen its ties with the sponsoring body, and this fear has proved reasonable enough in some cases. It is for the Group to prove, by its loyalty to the sponsoring body and its active support to the work, that such fears will be groundless.

If it is felt that this difficulty may be overcome by building on land belonging to the Sponsoring Authority, it must be remembered that it is hardly ever possible to buy the freehold of such land, and that any building erected upon it becomes the property of the owner when any lease or tenancy agreement expires. It may well be felt that, if the money to build the headquarters has been raised by the efforts of the Group, the premises should not pass to the sponsoring body and be used for non-Scout purposes in the event of the Group ceasing to exist. The only safe course is to find a plot of land of which the freehold can be secured by the Group.

It will probably always be the case that most sponsored Groups will meet in accommodation which belongs to the Sponsoring Authority, and will store their equipment there. For this reason, it is of vital importance that the provisions of P.O.R. 205 should be carefully followed. This rule provides that it should be decided what part of the equipment belongs to the Group itself, and what belongs to the Sponsoring Authority, and that this decision should be recorded in a letter of agreement between the G.S.M. and the Sponsoring Authority. If this is not done, it is very doubtful if the Group will be able to prove, in any legal sense, what belongs to it, if any dispute arises. There are a number of cases on record in which a dispute has caused the Group to withdraw from, or be denied access to, the accommodation which it has used, and the whole of the equipment has been taken over by the Sponsoring

Authority. Unless the Group had this letter of agreement by which they could prove what belonged to it, the equipment could only be recovered if the Sponsoring Authority was willing to release it.

So a sponsored Group has two steps to take: —

(i) to draw up a letter of agreement with the Sponsoring Authority, showing what belongs to whom;

(ii) to make the equipment which belongs to the Group the subject of a properly constituted Trust, as discussed in Chapter 8.

The Group's equipment varies from year to year, and the letter of agreement may easily get out of date, unless precautions are taken. The easiest way is to enter the details of the equipment on a schedule attached to the letter, and to revise the schedule when substantial alterations are necessary, and in any case once a year. This should not prove difficult, as similar particulars are required to be supplied to the Local Association every year, and are needed for the purposes of insurance and the Trust Deed. If the schedule, as so revised, is initialled both by the Sponsoring Authority and the G.S.M., the business is quite simply rounded off.

Church Groups

By far the largest number of sponsored Groups are attached to Churches; in fact, nearly half the total number in this country. The preceding pages of this chapter apply to all sponsored Groups, but certain special points relating to Church Groups must now be dealt with.

The religious policy of the Scout Movement is explained in detail in the booklet "Scouting, Religion and the Churches," a copy of which has been distributed to every Group. We are not always very good at seeing that a copy of this booklet, and of the "Sponsored Group" pamphlet, is supplied to a Sponsoring Authority, not only when a new Church Group is formed, but whenever there is a change of Sponsoring Authority. It should be the responsibility of the G.S.M. to see that this is done without fail, and to ask for an opportunity to discuss any points which the Sponsoring Authority may wish to raise. In case of need, he should not hesitate to ask the District Commissioner to enter into the discussions, and cases may arise where it is desirable to ask for the help of the County Chaplain of that denomination.

RELIGIOUS TRAINING

This is the responsibility of the Sponsoring Authority, under P.O.R. 180(4), and the G.S.M. must see that the members of the Group know what the rules of the Church are in this respect, and do their best to carry them out. The ideal situation is one in which the Scouters are themselves instructed members of the Church, and able and willing to help the Sponsoring Authority in religious teaching, but where this is not possible, they must at least do nothing to hinder *Scouts* from attending Church and Sunday School. On his side, the Sponsoring Authority will recognise the great value of the practical teaching of the Scout Law and Promise as an aid to his work.

Rules as to Church attendance are also for the Sponsoring Authority to settle, under P.O.R. 10(2). Conditions vary widely, but a few words may be said about

CHURCH PARADES

There must be a clear understanding between the Sponsoring Authority and the G.S.M. in this matter. In some Churches it is the custom to hold a monthly Church parade, perhaps in conjunction with the Girl Guides, and to make some acknowledgment of the presence of the young people by a special address suited to them. There is much virtue in a parade of this kind, as a corporate witness by the Group in uniform of the claims of the Church, so long as it is clearly understood that this is not the only occasion on which the boys come to Church. At other times, they come with their families, or on their own, and it is a great help if they know that they will find their Scouters there, too.

A friend of mine writes: " Clergy who wait calmly till a Troop is well established, and encourage the Scouters judiciously, will probably get an increase in congregation in the long run, but if they immediately get fussed about possibly losing a couple of choirboys on two or three summer afternoons, they just upset the apple-cart before the apples have been put in."

SCOUTS' OWNS

These were mentioned on pages 111-112. It need only be added that there is virtue in the holding of Scouts' Owns in Church Groups also, if the Sponsoring Authority agrees. It is a definite help to many boys to meet in this simple way to worship God in Scout surroundings, and a Scouts' Own may be regarded as something extra which a boy does for God because he is a Scout and has taken the Scout Promise. It need not be held on a Sunday.

Cases have been known where attendance at a regular weekly Scouts' Own has been agreed as equivalent to attendance at Sunday School, but this can only happen where one or more of the Scouters is qualified as a Sunday School teacher and is prepared to have a weekly meeting. It has the advantage that it enables teaching to continue even when the boys are in camp.

CO-OPERATION

The Scout and Guide Movements have issued a joint leaflet, entitled " Integration of Scout and Guide Units into the life of the Church," and this should be studied by Sponsoring Authorities and G.S.M.s. It is also highly desirable to consult with the Guide Authorities on these matters, and to reach agreement on a common policy. The suggestions made in the leaflet are designed to help " each boy and girl to have the maximum opportunity of becoming a worshipping and responsible member of the Church and a witness to it in their daily lives." The leaflet itself should be read and discussed in full, but a few points from it may be emphasised here.

(i) The Minister and Church officials can be of great help by taking an active interest in the affairs of the Group, and by making its members feel at home in the Church community.

(ii) Some of the Scouters can be office-bearers in the Church or members of the Parochial Church Council or similar body.

(iii) *Scouts* can be encouraged to play a more active part in the life of the Church by working for it in ways suitable to their ages.

(iv) Scouters should be recognised as fully occupied with the responsible job of training *Scouts*, and should not be expected to do all sorts of other Church jobs as well.

(v) *Scouts* should not be expected to undertake forms of service to their Church, or join in joint activities with other organisations, which would interfere with their basic *Scout* training.

SCOUTERS

It has already been suggested that the Sponsoring Authority himself has not usually got the time to carry out the full duties of G.S.M. It is, however, most desirable that he should be recognised by the boys as having an official position in the Group, and that he should pay them fairly regular visits. The position of Chaplain seems most suitable. The G.S.M. will, of course, see that the Sponsoring Authority is made welcome at Group events such as Investitures, Going-up Ceremonies, presentations of warrants and parents' evenings, and is given good notice of them.

As regards all the other Scouters, the Sponsoring Authority is responsible for nominating them to the D.C. and L.A., and this should never be a mere formality. They should come from the congregation, and be full members of the Church, regular in attendance and giving leadership by their example. It is a sad thing that Sponsoring Authorities have so often to confess that they cannot find a suitable person, but we must accept the fact. Where that is the case, and the G.S.M. finds someone who does not fulfil the above conditions, it must be recognised that trouble may arise at some time. The least the Movement can ask is that the Sponsoring Authority should fully satisfy himself that the candidate is not unsuitable from his point of view, and that the candidate himself should accept the necessity for loyalty to the conditions laid down by the Church for membership of the Group.

BOYS

Under P.O.R. 180 (1), the Sponsoring Authority has the broad duty of deciding what boys shall be admitted into the Group. He may not, except by special agreement with the D.C. and L.A., admit boys who belong to another Church or denomination. This rule will not usually be disregarded in a town, where boys of other Churches can usually find a Group to join, but in some smaller places an exception can be made, where the ministers of other denominations agree. If this arrangement is made, boys of other denominations must not be expected to attend a Church other than their own. It is usually desirable, however, for a Group in such a place to be registered as open.

But there is nothing in the rule to prevent a Church-sponsored Group from admitting boys of no religious attachment. As the Manpower Report stated: " Scouting can often be a bridge between the boy and the Church, and through becoming a Scout many a boy has entered into the family of the Church." It is the hope of the Movement that Church obligations such as membership of the choir or Sunday School will not be required as a prerequisite to membership of a Group. " Scouting should not be held out as a prize, or restricted to boys who are already good Church members." At the same time, it must be expected that " boys who join a Church-sponsored Group should be told plainly when they join what the Church and the Group will expect of them in the future," and the parents should understand the position from the outset.

Once the principle of admission has been agreed with the Sponsoring Authority, he will usually be content to leave the admission of individual boys with the G.S.M. and the section leaders, with whom it rests under P.O.R. 197 (i). The dismissal of a Scout is rather different. It is right that the G.S.M.'s approval should be necessary before a boy is dismissed (P.O.R. 197 (ii)), and that the boy should be given the right of appeal to the L.A. and D.C. (P.O.R. 197 (iii)). In such a case, the L.A. and D.C. must be careful to inform the Sponsoring Authority and to give him the opportunity to be heard. It is to be hoped that such cases are rare in the extreme, and that the G.S.M., sensing trouble, will let the Sponsoring Authority know what is happening and with him seek the right solution.

School Groups

Little need be said here about Groups sponsored by schools of various types. Their special problems are dealt with in two pamphlets, "Scouting in Preparatory Schools" and "Scouting in Secondary Schools," and schoolmasters can always obtain advice from the Commissioner for Education at I.H.Q.

School Groups should stick to the rules relating to ordinary Groups, and should see that their boys get the full *Scout* training, as far as possible. (P.O.R. 212 (ii) deals with this.) Any temptation in a residential school to make Scouting compulsory for the sake of uniformity or easy programme-planning must be sternly resisted.

The setting-up of a Scout Group in a non-residential school is sometimes resisted locally, on the ground that some of the best boys may be lured away from existing Groups in the place, but experience shows that where a school Group is started there are usually plenty of boys anxious to join from outside the Movement, without poaching on other Groups, whose Scouters will legitimately resent having boys stolen from them in this way. (I heard, for example, of a school Scoutmaster who obtained the names and addresses of boys who were to join the school in the following term, and who called upon the parents suggesting that the boys should join the school Troop, whether or not they already belonged to another Group!) But with proper behaviour, there need be no undesirable competition between school and other Groups, and there is usually plenty of room for both.

Handicapped Groups

The success of *Scout* methods among handicapped boys in hospitals and institutions makes it a matter of regret that there are not a larger number of Groups to deal with them. Such Groups exist in hospitals, schools for the blind and deaf, institutions for the mentally defective, and similar centres. Advice on this rather specialised subject can be obtained from the " Handbook of Handicapped Scouting," and from the Commissioner for Handicapped Scouts at I.H.Q.

While the Scouters of such Groups must be men or women with special sympathy for the work, they need not be doctors or nurses. Indeed, it is usually found that the best Scouters are those who come in from outside to run the Group, rather than members of the staff. Their value is largely due to the fact that they come from the outside world, and bring a refreshing atmosphere of normality into the artificial conditions of the hospital or institution. Someone of very senior standing, such as the Matron or Medical Superintendent, is usually the Sponsoring Authority, and much depends upon their sympathy and understanding. Some of the staff should be members of the Group Committee.

CHAPTER 12

THE SECTIONS OF THE GROUP

IT is clearly impossible, within the limits of a book of this kind, to discuss the methods of running a Cub Pack or Scout Troop. There is, fortunately, ample technical literature available. All that I can do is to draw attention to some of the matters to which the G.S.M. should devote his supervision, and especially those that involve the co-ordination of the work of the sections. That is the G.S.M.'s job, as we have already seen—to manage Scouters and not *Scouts*.

While the G.S.M. is not expected to be a technical expert, he is required by the terms of his appointment to have a general knowledge of the basic books—"Scouting for Boys," "The Wolf Cub's Handbook," "Rovering to Success," P.O.R., and current Senior Scout literature (which means, I take it, at the time of writing the pamphlet "Over 15" and "The Senior Scout Handbook"). Only by such general knowledge can he be sure that the Founder's ideas of progressive training suitable to the age of the boy are being carried out in the Group. The whole of this book centres round this idea of progress, and it is only the G.S.M. with no other duties in the Group who can bring an impartial mind to bear on it. All the other Scouters are bound to look at it from the viewpoint of their section.

Inevitably, therefore, in this chapter I must confine myself to a few points which strike me as important.

Let us consider first some of the problems of co-ordination, before passing on to special points relating to each section.

The G.S.M.'s visits

Whether he wants to turn out at night or not, the G.S.M.

must clearly be a fairly regular visitor to each of the sections of the Group, not only in the interests of proper supervision, but also because it is vital to the interests of the Group that the boys should know the G.S.M. and look up to him as the head of the family. But he must beware of two temptations. The first temptation is to forget that the running of the Troop is the Scoutmaster's job, and that the G.S.M. must not take over the programme, even though he may feel with some justification that he could run it better. From which it follows that he must never criticise the Scoutmaster in front of the boys. The second temptation is to be over-hearty with the boys themselves, particularly if it results in any lessening of smartness and discipline when on parade. It is natural for him to want to be on easy terms with the boys, and many G.S.M.s manage it admirably, but it can be overdone. It is salutary for a G.S.M. who may be getting on in years to remember that the Cub or young Scout believes that the old man is on his last legs—well into his eighties or nineties!—and is willing to give him the rather distant respect which is due to one so antiquated. Such a G.S.M. may be likened to grandfather, who is very welcome when he comes to visit the family, so long as he doesn't spoil the children and make them naughtier than usual.

The G.S.M. will be on such terms with the Scouters that he can drop in at any time without notice, perhaps towards the end of the evening when he can combine a social visit to the Troop or Pack with a little business with the Scoutmaster or Cubmaster after the boys have gone. He will not expect to be asked to take part in the programme, and will no doubt express surprise if asked to do so, but, like the singer who happens to have brought his music to the party, he will have something ready for the emergency—a game or a story carefully chosen as suitable to the section he is visiting.

But there are occasions when the G.S.M. should be expected to be present, and should be consulted as to dates.

These are the ceremonial occasions in the life of the Group or section—investitures, going-up ceremonies, presentations of warrants, Church parades (in a sponsored Group), and social events such as parents' evenings—at which it is the bounden duty of the G.S.M. to be present. It is well to have a standing arrangement as to the part which the G.S.M. should play in the ceremonies, for as the head of the Group he should certainly have a part to play. In a Cub investiture, for example, the G.S.M. may put the scarf round the boy's neck, for the scarf, being the same for all sections, is a symbol of the unity of the Group. At a going-up ceremony, the Cubmaster may hand the Cub over to the G.S.M., who in turn hands him over to the Scoutmaster—again a symbolic action the meaning of which will not be lost on the boys. But these are matters of choice, to be decided within the Group itself, subject to the general principle that the G.S.M. must not usurp the position of the section leader, nor on the other hand be left out in the cold.

If, as we may hope, the G.S.M. is notified of visits to the sections by the District Commissioner or one of his Assistants, it is both courteous and useful for the G.S.M. to be present if he can. I am referring here to the more formal type of Commissioner's visit, when he takes a serious look at programme, records, etc., and not to the casual " look in."

The G.S.M.'s visits to the Troop in camp are dealt with on page 158.

Admissions and Discharges

While the admission of a boy into the Group rests with the G.S.M. (P.O.R. 197 (i)), in normal circumstances he will not want to be consulted in every case, but will leave the decision to the section leader. It is wise to have an understanding with the section leaders as to the types of case which they should refer to the G.S.M. If I were a G.S.M., I should like to be consulted in cases of handicapped boys, boys who have been in trouble or are on probation, and, most certainly, all boys under the proper age, and those who wish to transfer from another Scout Group or another boys' organisation.

In the case of a sponsored Church Group, as already indicated in the chapter on sponsored Groups, the Sponsoring Authority will normally have a general understanding with the G.S.M. as to the admission of boys who are not Church members, but will leave individual cases to his discretion. For this reason, the G.S.M. should personally consider each case, in consultation with the section leader concerned.

It may happen that a boy who is a foreign subject applies to join the Group. In such a case, special procedure is necessary (P.O.R. 25). The District Commissioner's approval must be obtained, and the boy's name and address must be sent to the International Commissioner at I.H.Q. for record, together with the name of any foreign Group of which he was a member. He makes or re-affirms the Scout Promise in the following form:—

"On my honour I promise to do my best to do my duty to God, and to the country in which I am living; to help other people at all times; to obey the Scout Law."

More care is needed if the regrettable necessity arises of discharging a boy. To discharge him is to admit that we have given up hope of meeting his needs through the Group, and everything should be tried before proceeding to extremes. For this reason, the G.S.M.'s approval is necessary in every case (P.O.R. 197(ii)), and the *Scout* has the right of appeal to the Local Association and District Commissioner. It is their duty to consult the Sponsoring Authority in the case of a sponsored Group, and to hold an enquiry into the circumstances. At this enquiry the boy (and the Sponsoring Authority, if any) is entitled to be heard (P.O.R. 197(iii)). Such an appeal is rare in the extreme, but the procedure is there, in order to prevent injustice, and must be borne in mind by the careful G.S.M.

when he is considering the necessity for the discharge of any boy.

Transfers

Something has already been said, on pages 46-47, as regards the transfer of Scouters who move away from the Group. The same principle applies where *Scouts* move, namely that every effort should be made to see that the boy does not leave the Movement when he moves. A little personal trouble taken by the G.S.M. or section leader may be amply repaid later on. There is an official form (T 1) for use in such a case, and if it can be sent on its way before the boy actually moves, it will be easier for the receiving District to make him welcome without delay. The boy is often shy about making a new start in strange surroundings, but a call by a Scouter or a Patrol Leader will help him to overcome his shyness very quickly.

Any personal details about a boy's individual characteristics which are not provided for on form T 1 can be included in a covering letter. I.H.Q. will forward the form where the home Group does not know where to send it.

Special arrangements are made where a boy is migrating with his parents, or indeed without them. The form T 1 is sent to the Overseas or International Department at I.H.Q., as the case may be, and the name of the ship and the date of sailing should be shown, if possible. Another copy of the form should be given to the boy. I.H.Q. will forward the form to the country concerned, and the Scout authorities there will try to put him into touch with a Group immediately on arrival.

On the other side of the picture, everybody in the Group should be on the look-out for newcomers to their neighbourhood. It may be that the transfer procedure has been overlooked at the other end.

Another aspect of the transfer problem needs care, for it is apt to cause trouble unless carefully handled. That is where a boy applies to join the Group, and it is found that he is a member of another boys' organisation, or wants to transfer from another Scout Group. It behoves us all to play fair with our neighbours, and not take a boy from them because we are able to provide better facilities, or because the boy has had a difference of opinion with his leader. P.O.R. 199 lays down the procedure: "No boy may be accepted as a member of a Group within two months of his leaving another Group or another recognised boys' organisation, without a written approval of the transfer by the G.S.M. of his former Group (form T1), or by the proper authority of the other organisation. In case of dispute as to a transfer, the matter must be referred to the District Commissioner for decision."

Progressive Scouting

One of the G.S.M.'s most important jobs of co-ordination in a Group is to see that every boy is making progress, or at least is given every opportunity of doing so. One of the main causes of loss of keen boys is that they feel frustrated in their efforts to get on. At the time of writing, it is a fact that 80 per cent of Scouts between 11 and 15 years of age are still at Tenderfoot stage. It is obvious that an overhaul of Group machinery is necessary in many cases, and the G.S.M. should settle down to it with the Group Council. And here I would emphasise once again that where there is no separate G.S.M., one of the section leaders must always act as G.S.M. and take the lead in general problems involving more than one section.

We need to see that within each section progress is being made, and the progress charts obtainable from the Scout Shops help to keep the boys alive to the position. Only too often, boys are hung up because the Scouter is too busy to test them in the numerous parts of First and Second Star, Second and First Class. There are, for example, thirteen parts of the Second Class badge test. If eight boys are at that stage, the Scouter has 104 tests to examine. No wonder things get held up. But the rules do not insist that the

Scouter should do all the examining himself, and it is surely possible to get help from Senior Scouts, Rovers, Old Scouts and parents, where the Scouter is working single-handed.

In the Scout Troop, the Court of Honour can be asked to lay down a standard for the members of the Troop. It may, for example, be expected that a Scout should get his Second Class badge by 31st March unless he joined the Troop after 30th September. This gives the boy, and his Patrol Leader, a definite aim, even if the slowest boys cannot always get there by the given date.

In measuring progress, we are apt to think in terms of technical progress, First to Second Star, Second to First Class, and to overlook the far more important progress in the practice and understanding of the Law and Promise. Here I would like to quote what the Chief Scout wrote to Commissioners in 1952, altering only "King's Scout" in his letter to "Queen's Scout": —

"Second Star, Second Class, First Class, Queen's Scout, mark the progress so far as badges are concerned, and we have shown how the Cub, by concentrating on those badges which lead to Queen's Scout, can be encouraged to keep his eyes firm fixed on the goal. We are making some progress in this direction, but are we sure that our Scouts are making progress in the other side? Does their conception of the Law and the Promise progress, or do we mistake the means for the end? For the small boy, honour is a romantic ideal; for the Queen's Scout it should be recognised as the basis of civilisation, the barrier between the Dark Ages and the Brotherhood of Man. The Tenth Scout Law, too, although couched in the same words, should have a very different meaning for the boy as he passes from Tenderfoot to manhood. 'Duty to God' in the Promise probably means to most Cubs saying 'Thank You' to a kind old man with a beard who lives in a place called heaven beyond the skies, but, if we have not failed in *our* duty, by the time that Cub reaches Queen's Scout, religious experience should already be a fact, and the Power and the Glory be revealed.

" This spiritual development, the growth of the divinity that lies deep in every small boy's heart, is just as much a requirement for Second and First Class and Queen's Scout as any of the other tests. It is the most important test of all."

Loss of boys

The Scout Movement has talked about " leakage," or loss of boys, ever since I can remember—and still it goes on. One reason is the lack of progressive Scouting, as indicated in the previous paragraphs, but there are a number of others, and it is clearly the job of the G.S.M. and Group Council to see that the avoidable loss is reduced to a minimum.

There will always be some loss, if only because some boys just come into Scouting to see what it is like, and find they don't like it, even in a perfectly good Troop or Pack. Others, as they grow older, find that they cannot face up to the responsibility of the Law and Promise. Still others move away, and don't take up Scouting again.

But when all excuses are made, many more boys are lost owing to some fault inside the Movement itself. Lack of imagination and adventure in the programme is often the cause—a succession of routine meetings indoors, with the boy knowing perfectly well what to expect. Too many pointless games, and too little purposeful work. Lack of smartness and discipline. Little or no use of the Patrol system.

All these things need studying week by week in the Group itself, for they will differ from Group to Group. The annual census figures, looked at over a period of two or three years, can be a help, but they can also be deceptive. Numbers may remain steady or even increase, but are the boys at the beginning and end of the year the same boys, or has there been a large turnover of boys leaving and of others coming in and leaving in their turn?

Full, frank and Scoutlike discussion of the whole business by the Group Council is needed in order to get at the facts of loss, the reason why each boy left, and then to hammer out the remedy, however unwelcome it may be to an individual Scouter. Two recent examples come to my mind as showing how the Scouters of all sections can help, even though the particular problem may not arise in their own section. In the first case, a Scout of 14½ who had been an excellent Cub Sixer and a good member of the Troop left. The Scoutmaster was busy and did not immediately go round and see the boy to find out why. But the lady who had been the boy's Cubmaster heard of it, and was horrified to hear that one of her best boys had left the Troop, and she called on him to know the reason why. After a bit of dodging, the boy came out with it—he wanted to be a Senior Scout along with his pals. It was a good Group, and the G.S.M. and S.M.(S) were sensible people, who knew that P.O.R. was intended to be a help rather than a hindrance, so they popped him into the Senior Scout Troop, where he has settled in quite happily again.

In the other case, the Cubmaster complained that nearly all her Cubs left soon after going up into the Troop. She kept her head and temper, raised the matter at the Group Council and asked for guidance. Was her training in the Pack wrong, or was something wrong in the Troop? After a full discussion, the Group Council decided that the fault lay in the Troop, and the Scoutmaster resigned—which was, in fact, just what was needed. (This case, by the way, was another example of the value of a separate G.S.M., who could take an impartial attitude.)

If you feel any doubt about the magnitude of this problem, consider these figures. Between 1946 and 1953, Cubs increased by some 50,000, whereas Boy Scouts of 11-15 *decreased* by some 5,000!

Good Turns

The general public, so ignorant of most Scouting affairs, has caught on to the idea that " all Scouts do a good deed every day." As usual, they have got it a bit wrong, and some Scouters seem to be a bit wrong, too. It is the Cub who undertakes to " do a good turn to somebody every day "; the Scout is at the more advanced stage of promising to " help other people at all times." In this, as in all else, Scouting must be progressive. The small boy starts by looking out for one good turn a day. As his eyes are opened, he gets more observant and finds more than one—finds them cropping up all over the place, in fact—until at Senior Scout and Rover age the lad has developed an unalterable habit of service to others.

At first, the small boy needs a lot of help. The idea is new to him, and needs to be explained with homely examples that he can understand when he first joins the Pack—or the Troop, if he has not been a Cub. Suggestions for good turns should be made to him, until he has got the idea, and discreet enquiries made, out of earshot of the rest of the boys, as to what success he has found in looking out for things to do and then doing them.

It is one thing to be willing to do a good turn, it is quite another to be able to perform it. The Cub may want to help his small sister when she cuts her finger, but he can only be effective if he knows how to " clean and dress a cut finger." Passing his First and Second Star tests, and remembering what he has passed, enables him to do his good turns efficiently.

Patrols should be encouraged to look out for good turns which will involve the whole Patrol. And from time to time and particularly at Christmas, the whole Group should be busy on a Group good turn on a big scale for people less fortunate than themselves—folks in hospitals, old folk, or young folk from poor homes.

Two more points may be mentioned. Firstly, some people seem to think that Scouts are useful in order to save them trouble or money, and G.S.M.s must be careful to see that their boys are not being exploited, nor their training interfered with. Secondly, let us be quite sure that our *Scouts* realise their obligation to do even more good turns, just because in Bob-a-job week they ask the public to pay them for their work.

Saluting

I am sure that many Groups need to pay far more attention than they do to the subject of the *Scout* salute. P.O.R. 352-353 are worth studying, and any Group which wishes to be smart should train its *Scouts* accordingly. Establish a tradition for smartness in this respect—the boys like it. Moreover, occasions for saluting frequently occur when the Group is in the public eye, and we are often very justifiably criticised for being sloppy.

The main reason underlying the *Scout* salute is often not realised; indeed, some people seem to think it is a tribute owed by an inferior to a superior. But the Founder explained it very simply in " Scouting for Boys ": "A salute is merely a sign between men of standing. It is a privilege to be able to salute anyone. In the old days the freemen of England were all allowed to carry weapons, and when one met another each would hold up his right hand to show that he had no weapon in it, and that they met as friends. . . . To salute merely shows that you are a right sort of fellow and mean well to the others; there is nothing slavish about it."

So the first use of the salute is as a greeting. As the rule says, " *Scouts*, Scouters, persons holding non-executive or honorary rank, meeting for the first time in the day, salute each other. The first to see the other should be the first to salute, irrespective of rank. *Scouts* and *Guides* salute each other when in uniform." But how few of us, boys or men, really do this. One reason is that a great many *Scouts* fail to wear their buttonhole badge in ordinary clothes. Now, the badge is not only a reminder to the *Scout* that he is a *Scout* all day long, whether in uniform or not, but it is also the only means of recognising a brother *Scout* in the street. There is urgent need for Groups to establish a tradition in both these respects—that all should wear their *Scout* badge in mufti and that all should make a point of trying to be the first to see another *Scout* and give him the salute, as a sign of greeting, accompanied by a cheerful grin. All except Cubs can use the Scout sign (right hand level with the shoulder, palm to the front, and fingers as in the salute) as a greeting if they so wish.

Salutes are also given as a token of respect—at the hoisting of the National flag, at the playing of the National anthem, to Scout flags other than Patrol flags, and to funerals. All members of the Group should know what to do on such occasions, as set out in P.O.R. 353, and this applies to Cubs as well as to everyone else. In my experience, they rarely know what to do on public occasions. Two main points need to be borne in mind: (i) in Church, *Scouts* do not salute, but stand at the alert; (ii) on all public parades, other than in Church, the leader calls the *Scouts* to the alert and he alone salutes. These two points apply to all such occasions, except when the *Scout* Promise is being made or re-affirmed, in which case Cubs give the full salute and all others the Scout sign.

Cubs always want to take their caps off during the playing of the National anthem. They should practise the proper procedure in the Pack.

*　　*　　*

These points are but a few of those in which the G.S.M.'s supervision is necessary in order to ensure co-ordination and progress, but they are all concerned with the Group as a whole. Many others appear in other chapters.

We now consider a few matters relating to each section, and affecting the G.S.M.'s own job.

THE WOLF CUB PACK

Atmosphere

The atmosphere of a good Cub Pack is quite unique, and certainly very different from that of any other section of the Group. It is founded on the Jungle Book stories of Kipling, and the G.S.M. will be wise if he reads them, if he has not done so already. How otherwise can he understand why the Cub gives in to the Old Wolf, why the Cubmaster is not Miss Smith or Ma'am, but Akela, and why he himself should submit to such a name as Hathi the Elephant without protest?

But while the Jungle Book forms the foundation, there can and should be other kinds of romance, sometimes changing with bewildering speed from Robin Hood to a Fire Brigade. And, at the same time, romance will be dropped for short periods of serious work, for a Pack that is all play and no work is a failure.

All this the G.S.M. can absorb from "The Wolf Cub's Handbook" and other textbooks, and one thing at least will be clear to him, that Cubbing is not watered-down Scouting. Sixes there are, and Sixers, to lead in games and help with their example, but they are nothing like Scout Patrols and Patrol Leaders. If he ventures into the Sixers' Council, he will not be alarmed by some of the Sixers' fantastic suggestions, for it has no powers of government such as the Court of Honour has.

At least the G.S.M. must know enough to avoid appearing grossly ignorant to the Pack. However frightened he may be, he must march into the middle of the circle when the Pack wishes to give him the Grand Howl, and remember to salute, with two fingers, after the leading Sixer has called "Dyb, dyb, dyb, dyb."

Size of the Pack

The size of the Pack may cause him some concern, for most good Packs in urban areas have waiting-lists, and it is a temptation to enlarge a Pack beyond a manageable size. P.O.R. 218 lays it down that a Pack must not exceed 36 in number, but 24 is a much better maximum, and a Cubmaster and two Assistants is the minimum staff even for that number. Remember, there can be two Packs in one Group.

The Old Wolves

It is very desirable to have both sexes represented among the Old Wolves. In most Packs, the Cubmaster will be a lady, but at least one man is needed to get the right balance, and particularly to look after the older Cubs, who are reaching the age when they start to look to a man for leadership.

Instructors

Where a Group is short of Old Wolves, Cub Instructors can most usefully fill the gap. They may be adults who do not feel they have the time to accept a warrant, Girl Guides or Rangers (if the Guide authorities permit), Scouts, Senior Scouts or Rovers. But care must be taken to see that a Scout is not allowed to become an Instructor until his own training is fairly advanced. He must have reached the age of 15 or hold the First Class Badge (P.O.R. 225). Moreover, a girl who is not a member of the Guide Movement may become an Instructor. At the age of 16 (but not before that age), she may start a probationary period of six months, and should then be expected to take the Scout Promise. Many of such girls have done excellent work, and have gone on to accept warrants as A.C.M.s when they reach 18.

Under-age Cubs

Some soft-hearted and soft-headed Cubmasters are inclined to take boys under the age of eight, and invent all sorts of ingenious excuses for the practice. But G.S.M.s must be adamant in refusing to countenance it. The Cub programme is not designed to last more than three years, and the older Cubs hate having infants under their feet.

Loss at going-up age

There has always been a heavy loss of Cubs at going-up age, and some of it is inevitable. It is the job of the G.S.M. and Group Council to see that it is as small as they can continue to make it. The proper going-up age for the normal boy is 11, but by agreement between Cubmaster and Scoutmaster it can be extended beyond that age and up to 12 where it seems to be in the interest of a particular boy, but not because the Cubmaster finds her Sixers so useful! It is Akela's job to prepare the Cub for his going-up, and to keep the whole Pack interested in what the Troop is doing. But not even the best Akela can interest the Pack in a rotten Troop.

The Scoutmaster and the Patrol Leaders have a big part to play. They must be interested enough to visit the Pack from time to time, so that they are known to the Cubs and (we hope) liked by them. When a Cub is nearly ready to go up, he can learn his Tenderfoot tests from the S.M. and his future P.L. while still in the Pack, so that his investiture as a Scout can follow immediately after the going-up ceremony. And if the C.M. has persuaded the parents to save up for his Scout uniform before he goes up, he can wear it for his investiture and look the same as the rest of the Troop.

The first month or two in the Troop is critical, and the welcome given him by the Troop makes all the difference. He is entitled to consideration, for he has already been enrolled as a member of the world-wide brotherhood—perhaps three years ago—and is that much ahead of a boy who has not been a Cub.

If the Group is in close touch with the boy's parents, as it should be, they can be of the greatest help in easing the going-up strain. They need to appreciate that Cubbing is not an end in itself, but the gateway to real Scouting. Moreover, they should be consulted about the change in hours, for one week their son may be returning from his Pack meeting about eight o'clock, while the next week he strolls home from Scouts at nine-thirty or ten.

Change of school, and consequent increase of homework, also need to be provided for.

Lastly, the G.S.M. should pay particular attention to the going-up ceremony. It is almost the only occasion on which Troop and Pack meet, and the bearing and behaviour of the Scouts have an important effect, not only on the Cub who is going up, but on the whole Pack. This is one occasion when Scout discipline must be rigid, for why should the Cubs feel an ambition to enter the Troop if the Scouts seem to be laughing at them or to be bored or restless?

THE BOY SCOUT TROOP

(This section deals with the Boy Scout Troop consisting of boys between 11 and 15. Those over 15 are discussed in the next section.)

The Scout Troop is quite different in atmosphere from the Cub Pack. The boy has reached the age when he wants to *do* things; the age of pretence is past. He wants adventure, fun and enterprise, camping and the outdoor life, and will leave unless he gets them.

As pointed out on pages 134-135, the Boy Scout Troop needs special attention, because far too many boys leave it at far too early an age. It is the section for which the Founder wrote " Scouting for Boys," and all else in Scouting is complementary to it.

The Troop and the Patrols

In the past, too much emphasis has been placed upon the Troop as a unit, and for many years it was the custom to describe it as divided into Patrols. The Patrol was thus given too little importance in the scheme. But P.O.R. 240 (i) now says "A Troop is composed of Patrols, each consisting of 6 to 8 Scouts, including the Patrol Leader and Second," and the second sub-paragraph makes the important statement: " The Patrol should be the unit in all activities." But is that so in practice?

In 1950, the Chief Scout wrote: "One thing that is disturbing me is the fact that we haven't yet got down to the Patrol system. Perhaps most of your Scouters would tell you that they are working to the Patrol system, but my own experience in talking to the boys is that very few really know the Patrol Leader's job and are doing it." Many Scouters do not realise what fundamental importance the Founder gave to the Patrol system. They should read the chapter on that subject in "Aids to Scoutmastership." Here are two quotations from it. "The Patrol system is the one essential feature in which Scout training differs from that of all other organisations, and where the system is properly applied it is absolutely bound to bring success, it cannot help itself." And again, "The Patrol is the unit of Scouting always, whether for work or play, for discipline or for duty."

Some other countries, notably Norway, use the Patrol system far more than is common in this country. Indeed, in that country, Troops often meet as seldom as once a month, and the weekly meetings are Patrol meetings. It is time we got down to this seriously.

The Patrol and the Patrol Leader

If the Patrol is the unit, the Patrol Leader has a far more responsible job than many of us admit. He is "appointed by the S.M., in consultation with the Court of Honour or the Patrol concerned; he trains his Patrol through activities at Troop and Patrol meetings and camps; he plans the activities for Patrol meetings and camps, with the assistance of his Second and subject to the advice of the S.M. and the Court of Honour" (P.O.R. 241). This involves two things: (i) the choice of the right boy as Patrol Leader, and (ii) the training of the P.L.s by the S.M., as he is bound to do under the terms of his appointment (P.O.R. 234 (iii)).

To quote the Chief Scout again: "Scouters will, I know, tell you that they haven't the time to train their Patrol

Leaders while training every boy in the Troop, but over and over again B.-P. emphasised that it wasn't their job to train every boy in the Troop." Time put into P.L. training will save an enormous amount of time in the end. This is a first priority for the G.S.M. and Troop Scouters in a Group which has not hitherto used the Patrol system to the full.

There is much to be said in favour of a Patrol consisting of boys of about the same age, so that they become a real "gang" (which at that age they love to be) and go about together in their spare time, getting out to the nearest bit of country or park to practise their Scouting at odd times. That is the best kind of Patrol meeting. But it is also a great advantage to have a den of their very own (see page 86).

The Troop Leader

It is not necessary to have a Troop Leader, but an outstanding Scout can do a valuable job in that rank. It is wise not to make such an appointment unless you have someone who possesses the full qualifications laid down in P.O.R. 238 (ii): ability to lead; age not less than 15; service as a Patrol Leader for at least six months; the First Class Badge; a general knowledge of "Scouting for Boys." Perhaps his most valuable functions are to set an outstanding example and to act as Chairman of the Court of Honour.

The Court of Honour

This is an essential part of the Patrol system. It consists of the Patrol Leaders and the Troop Leader, if any. In small Troops it is a good plan for Seconds also to attend, as part of their training. The Scoutmaster may attend, but strictly as an adviser. It is fatal if he tries to run the show or to dictate to the P.L.s. Other Scouters of the Troop should not attend, unless invited by the Chairman, who will normally be the Troop Leader or one of the P.L.s elected for the purpose. Another P.L. should act as Scribe to the Court, keep the minutes of the meetings, and see that the proper persons take action as required.

The Scoutmaster is bound to delegate as far as possible to the Court of Honour all internal matters of discipline and administration, including the expenditure of Troop funds raised by the Scouts themselves or allotted to them for current expenses by the Group Committee (P.O.R. 234 (ii)). The functions of the Court of Honour are therefore defined in P.O.R. 239 (ii) as follows: "The Court of Honour is responsible for guarding the honour of the Troop, for arranging the programme of Troop activities, and for internal administration. . . . It is also one of the methods by which Patrol Leaders are trained."

I particularly like the bit about guarding the honour of the Troop. The Court of Honour's chief function is to build up tradition, to set standards of achievement and progress, and to carry the Scout Promise and Law into the life of the Patrols and the Troop. Once that has been done, details of administration become easy.

The idea of arranging the programme of activities is that the Court says in general terms what the boys want to do in the next few months, while the S.M. takes these views into account in planning the detailed programme.

The Patrol in Council

It is the Patrol Leader's job to represent the views of his Patrol at the Court of Honour, on matters which they have discussed. Hence the usefulness of a meeting of all the Scouts in the Patrol, called the Patrol in Council (P.O.R. 242A), to discuss its affairs.

Scouts

It is perhaps worth repeating that special attention should be given to Cubs coming up from the Pack, while by no means neglecting the newcomer who has not been a Cub. First impressions count for so much, and the new arrival who isn't given anything special to do at his first Troop meeting except to be heaved around by bigger boys in

"British Bulldog" ("genial brutality," as I heard it described) must wonder whether it is worth coming again.

In particular, he should not be kept hanging about for months to be invested. If the ex-Cub has been passed in his Tenderfoot tests while still in the Pack, he should be invested not later than the week after his going-up ceremony. If the non-Cub is properly looked after, he should be able to pass his tests within a month. On no account should he be kept waiting a moment longer than is necessary after he has passed them.

At the other end of the scale, "a Scout on reaching the age of 15 must receive special training and treatment suitable to his years" (P.O.R. 244 (ii)). This applies in every case, whether or not the boy goes up to a Senior Troop in the Group, and even if he is a Patrol Leader with the responsibilities of a Patrol upon his shoulders. Where there is a Senior Troop or Patrol, the boy must have attained the age of 15 before going up, but there is nothing to say that he must go up precisely on his fifteenth birthday. A reasonable latitude, say up to 16, may be allowed, especially in the case of a Patrol Leader who may be needed for a short time to train his successor.

Preparation for work

The majority of boys in this country leave school and go to work soon after becoming 15. It is therefore the job of the Scoutmaster of the Boy Scout Troop to see that the boy who starts work at 15 does not enter upon it unprepared. We must try to prevent boys going to dead-end jobs. The Youth Employment Officer is always ready to advise, and parents whose sons have no ready-made employment should be recommended by the S.M. to consult that officer. Perhaps also the Group Committee can help to put some boys in the right places.

But it is also important that the boy should be prepared for the great change from a life which may have been somewhat sheltered to the rough world of industry or commerce, where his Scout standards will be challenged, perhaps for the first time. He must realise that this will be a real test of what the Law and Promise mean to him, and that the atmosphere and companionship of a Scout Troop will be of even greater value to him than when he was a schoolboy.

"OVER-15s" AND SENIOR SCOUTS

As we have seen already, a Scout on reaching the age of 15 must receive special training and treatment suitable to his years, but it is left to the discretion of the Group, in consultation with the District Commissioner, to decide whether the "over-15s" shall remain in the Boy Scout Troop, form a separate senior Patrol within that Troop, or be formed into a separate Senior Scout Troop.

There are no Senior Scout Troops in Scotland, but in the rest of the United Kingdom a majority of opinion is in favour of them, but only if the numbers are sufficient and if there is adequate and separate leadership. Figures seem to show that since 1945 the existence of Senior Scout Troops has succeeded in retaining a large number of boys in the Movement, but I will not argue the point here. The choice is, in England, in the hands of the Group.

The Local Association and District Commissioner will not allow a Group to develop a Senior Troop of more than one Patrol unless they are satisfied that a suitable Scouter is available who does not hold any other warrant in the Group, except if necessary that of G.S.M. (P.O.R. 247G), and who is not less than 25 years old. Any Assistant Scoutmaster of a Senior Troop must not be less than 21 (P.O.R. 247C(2)).

Possible dangers

The G.S.M. may have to watch for some possible dangers when a Senior Troop exists. It must be clear to all concerned—

(i) that there are enough boys between 13 and 15 in

the Boy Scout Troop to ensure continuity in the Senior Scout Troop;

(ii) that Senior Scouting should not be carried on at the expense of the other sections, financially and otherwise;

(iii) that there should not be a concentration on the physical toughness of the programme at the expense of mental and spiritual training.

Patrol System

The system of the Boy Scout Troop should not be slavishly imitated. In the Senior Troop, the Patrol generally consists of smaller numbers (from 4 to 7, including the Patrol Leader). It need not be the only unit for work or play, and *ad hoc* teams can be formed for special activities. The Scout method is evolving, as the boy grows older, from the Patrol as a unit to the ultimate aim, which is the responsibility of the individual.

But though the Patrol system is modified, the Court of Honour gains in importance. The Seniors will want to make their own decisions, and the Scoutmaster is far more of an adviser than he can be in the Boy Scout Troop. Where numbers are small, the whole Troop in Council may be used to reinforce the Court of Honour, or even to take its place until numbers increase.

Investiture

A boy becomes a Senior Scout by investiture, during which he re-affirms his Scout Promise (P.O.R. 247M). This marks the beginning of a new stage in his life, possibly just as he is leaving school and going to work, and should be marked with all proper ceremonial.

Even where there is no Senior Troop, the "over-15" should have this stage in his career marked by a suitable ceremony and should re-affirm his Promise (P.O.R. 244 (ii)).

In both cases, the boy must be expected to understand

the wider interpretation of the Promise which is appropriate to his age, and to be carrying it out in his daily life.

Programmes

The number of boys over 15 in the average Group is small, and the arrangement of programmes presents difficulties, especially when homework or evening school has also to be fitted in. Often, where there is no Senior Troop, there are only two or three boys of the 15-18 age range. In order to help with this difficulty, it is to be hoped that District Commissioners will see to it that a District programme is arranged, in which these isolated units can take part. A good Assistant Commissioner for Senior Scouts can do most valuable work by offering such a programme on (say) a monthly basis, and by making suggestions for activities in the intervening weeks by individual boys or small teams, perhaps in preparation for the next monthly event. But the rules make it clear that a Senior Troop for the whole District cannot be registered (P.O.R. 247Q (i)), for the boys must not be detached from their loyalty to their own Group.

Meetings of Senior Scouts should not always be in the Group Headquarters, and need not always be in uniform. An all-round programme of training may well include a visit to a good play or film, to the local Council Meeting, to see the local paper go to press, or what-not—especially when these outings are followed by discussion in the Troop. An occasional social affair to which girls are invited is also a part of Scout training. Perhaps it might be a Twelfth Night party, complete with party games and marvellous things to eat.

Special events

Any good Senior Troop hopes to have a Queen's Scout or two in its midst. It should be known by the Group Committee that a Queen's Scout has the privilege of receiving a Royal certificate from the hands of the Chief Scout himself. The Committee should be prepared to pay the expenses of attending such a reception, if the Local Association does not pay them itself.

World Jamborees take place every four years, and contingents from this country usually consist of boys over 15. It should be the ambition of the Group to get as many of its members included in the contingent as possible. Arrangements will need to be made well in advance to meet the expenses. But World Jamborees do not happen every year, and are sometimes in a distant Continent. Seniors should plan to go on a foreign trip at least every two or three years, so that every Senior has the chance of one such trip during his period between 15 and 18. These expeditions, valuable though they are, must not absorb so much of the Group's resources that the other sections are left short of money for essential purposes. It is a matter for arrangement with the Group Committee, and the possibility of grants from the Local Education Authority, or from I.H.Q., should not be overlooked.

Leaving the Troop

The time comes for the boy (now rising to young manhood) to leave the Troop. The rule is that he must leave not later than his eighteenth birthday, unless the District Commissioner specially authorises an extension (P.O.R. 244 (i) and 247N (ii)). Such an extension may usually be given to a lad who is going on his National Service soon after he reaches 18 and who wants to stay in the Troop until he goes.

Much depends upon whether the Group has an active Rover Crew, but the majority of Groups have not. The Rovers are naturally anxious to get the lad transferred to the Crew and settled into it before he goes on National Service, so the rules provide that, while the age of admission to a Crew is necessarily dependent on the physical and mental development of a boy in his progress to manhood, he must be at least 17 years of age and preferably 18

(P.O.R. 264 (3)). This can best be settled by the G.S.M. and Group Council in the light of the circumstances of the Group, the prime consideration being the well-being of the lad himself.

The B.-P. Guild of Old Scouts is there to receive him, if he is unable to become a Rover (see Chapter 14).

National Service

Many thousands of our young men go into their National Service direct from membership of a Scout Group. What does the Group do about it? It is part of the G.S.M.'s function " to ensure that contact is maintained with members of the Group serving in the Forces " (P.O.R. 173 (6)). We know that very many Groups maintain such contacts splendidly, but many others do not. This is quite inexcusable, and must be remedied.

Let us first of all recognise that one of our Scouts may be a conscientious objector. His conscience must be respected and the G.S.M. should know exactly what the policy of the Movement is in regard to such a Scout. The following declaration has been published: " The Chief Scout does not say that Scouts must in every case be prepared to join the Armed Forces, because he recognises that there are those who conscientiously object to taking life, but he does expect that all Scouters and *Scouts* shall be prepared to render National Service in some form. If a member of the Movement conscientiously objects to taking life, his Scout Promise of Duty to God, Queen and neighbours must compel him to render service in any other capacity to which he may be directed by H.M. Government.

" It is clear that one who is not prepared to give definite and practical service to his country cannot be a member of the Boy Scout Brotherhood. It is equally clear that one who attempts in any sense to dissuade others from doing their duty to their country cannot be a member of the Boy Scouts Association."

We owe it to the Scout who joins the Forces that he

should be properly briefed by whichever Scouter is most competent to do so, usually the G.S.M. or the Scouter with whom he is working at the time of call-up. Nothing can take the place of personal talks, but where this is difficult use can be made of a briefing pamphlet addressed to the lad, entitled "This is addressed to you," obtainable from I.H.Q. But no talk or pamphlet will do much good if the previous years of training have been inadequate. We must rely upon the effect of good Scouting, but we can impress upon the lad the opportunity with which he is now faced—to show what Scouting has done for him, and to make the most of the companionship and the broadening of experience which the Services may bring to him.

Before he goes, the Scout should be given by the Group a Service Scout wristlet badge and a Service Scout membership card—both obtainable through L.A. Badge Secretaries. And a little farewell party will not come amiss.

All three Services officially recognise our form R.S. (Record of Service) with which the Scout should be supplied before he goes. Supplies can be obtained from I.H.Q. The form, two copies of which he should take with him, gives his Scout history, including proficiency badges gained and experience of leadership, together with any special aptitudes and hobbies. The War Office has given instructions that the form shall be attached to his papers, and proceed with him from unit to unit throughout his Service life. Experience shows, alas, that few of these forms are in fact handed in, but whether this is because the Scouter does not fill them in or because the lad decides that his achievements in Scouting have been mediocre, I do not know.

It is the responsibility of someone in the Group to keep in touch with the lad all the time he is serving in the Forces, and to drop him a line from time to time, giving the Group events, news about other fellows on service, and so forth. Some Groups have a news-sheet which can be circulated, others send their absent friends copies of "The Scouter." A card at Christmas-time will be very welcome.

A few fellows are marked out as potential warrant-holders, and it is obviously most important to maintain contact with them. Where the G.S.M. is pretty certain about the lad, there is no reason why he should not get him a warrant before he goes. Application can be made to the D.C. and L.A. when he is 17 years, 8 months, so that he can start his probation then, and the warrant can be issued to him immediately he is 18 and before he is called up.

As to Scouting while he is in the Services, it is the endeavour of I.H.Q. to obtain a Service Scout Liaison Officer in all the main concentrations of the Army and R.A.F., who will put the lad in touch with local Scouting, arrange visits to Scout camps and other places of interest and pass his details on when he is posted elsewhere.

If he is posted to Western Europe, to the Middle East or the Far East, he may well find a Service Rover Crew which he can join.

As regards the Royal Navy, see the following paragraph.

Deep-Sea Rover Scouts

This branch of the Rover Scout section of the Movement is open to all serving seafarers, *i.e.* members of the Royal Navy, the Merchant Navy, the Fishing Fleets and the crews of ocean-going yachts. It is not confined to those who have been Sea Scouts, or to those who are doing their National Service. I need not go into details here, for a pamphlet is obtainable from I.H.Q., but I can testify to the value of the contacts which Deep-Sea Rovers are able to make with Scouting in ports all over the world, and all Scouts going to sea should be told about the Branch.

THE ROVER CREW

The Rover Scout section of the Movement is weak, when compared with the years before 1939. That is not a matter for surprise, in view of the demands of National Service just at the time when the young man would be planning to join a Rover Crew. Crews are, in general, small in numbers and are able to do little in the way of combined training and activities. Many of those who belong to Crews are also Scouters, or are busy studying and courting. About one Group in every three has a Crew.

Nevertheless, it should be the aim of the G.S.M. and the Group Council to form an active Crew, if possible, in order to complete the scheme of training and to provide useful service for the Group. Moreover, the example of a good Rover is an incentive to the younger members of the Group. But they are not impressed by a number of gentlemen who appear to their eyes well advanced in years, and who appear only seldom in the ranks of the Group.

It is, no doubt, true that some who call themselves Rovers are busy with jobs of service outside the Scout Movement and can spare little time for Scouting. At the risk of being controversial, I would express the view that the best place for these chaps is in the ranks of the Old Scouts, leaving the Rover Crew for young men who want to do some active work for Scouting. Any number of Scouters are still needed, and for those who do not feel drawn to work in a warranted capacity there are plenty of other jobs, such as Instructors, Badge Examiners, Quartermasters, Editors of Group magazines, and a score of others.

Composition of the Crew

The Crew is divided into three stages (P.O.R. 257): —

(i) Rover Squires—those in the probation stage (age 17 or preferably 18, but not over 23);

(ii) those in the training stage, after investiture as Rovers (under 25);

(iii) those in the service stage—the older members of the Crew, who have reached that stage by their 25th birthday and cease when they can no longer be active Rovers.

It is important that those in (iii) should not seek to interfere with the arrangement of the active Rover programme by those in the other two stages.

Leaders

There are certain special qualifications laid down for a Rover Leader (see pages 39-40).

In view of the shortage of Rover Leaders, extra importance attaches to the rank of Rover Mate, who is a Rover elected annually by the Crew. A number of good Rover Mates, with some help from an Assistant Commissioner for Rovers or a District Rover Scout Leader who can provide sufficient activities on a District basis, can carry on Crews quite efficiently.

Scouters as Rovers

Opinion is divided as to whether it is a good thing for a Scouter to be a Rover as well. P.O.R. 262 states the policy, namely that "a Rover may take up a warrant without ceasing to be a member of the Crew, but his duties as a Scouter must come first. The possession of a warrant will not give him any precedence as a Rover." It is natural that a young man who is already a member of a Crew and who then takes up a warrant should want to retain the companionship of his fellow-Rovers and to join in some of their activities, but he runs three dangers—one, that he may not have time to do both properly; two, that he may be tempted to go off on a jaunt with the Crew when his real duty is to his Troop or Pack; three, that he may be spending too much of his time in Scouting.

Rovers and Old Scouts

The B.-P. Guild of Old Scouts (see Chapter 14) has made it clear that it will not seek to lure Rovers away from active membership of Crews. At the same time, the Group will, it is hoped, have an Old Scout Branch for those of its "old boys" (some of them very old) who can no longer be active in Scouting, and the G.S.M. should give serious thought to the problem whether some elderly Rovers in the Crew should not be urged, gently but effectively, to leave the Crew and join the B.-P. Guild.

CHAPTER 13

CAMPING

CAMPING is the key activity of Scouts, and the Founder certainly led the way in showing what an important part camping can play in the training of boys. For this reason, I have given a separate chapter to this subject, for if we are to camp, we must camp well. Bad camping can do all sorts of damage—it is a danger to health and morale, it loses boys to Scouting, and it affects the good reputation of the Movement in the Troop's home neighbourhood and in the place where it camped.

A bad camp reflects upon the G.S.M.'s previous supervision of the arrangements and training of his Scouters, for it is his responsibility to see that the section leaders have the necessary experience and can be trusted to make proper use of it. An inexperienced Scouter should not be in charge of a camp until he has seen good camping, either in his own Group or under an experienced Scouter of another Troop.

The six fundamentals

The G.S.M.'s supervision should extend to the six points mentioned below: —

(i) Camping appropriate to the section should be carried out. There should be a progressive programme as the boy gets older. (The special circumstances of a Cub Pack are considered below.) Generally speaking, the Boy Scout camp should develop into the treks and hikes of the Senior Scouts and the Rovers.

Camping is the great opportunity for the Scouter to get to know his boys, and it is an implied condition of his getting a warrant that he should be prepared to camp with the boys. It is often in camp that he learns how best to deal with a difficult boy when they return home. Moreover, in camp so much training can be done, not only in outdoor subjects which are difficult to practise in towns, but also in discipline and the full use of the Patrol system. For this reason, Patrol rather than central cooking is strongly recommended.

Patrol camps can be run, usually at week-ends, without Scouters, but only if the Scouters have previously given the necessary training to the Patrol Leaders.

Winter camps are all right for Senior Scouts and Rovers, but youngsters—especially those going to their first camp—are better off if they wait until Whitsun. This leaves Easter as a good opportunity for a training camp for Patrol Leaders and Seconds.

(ii) Agreement should be reached on the Group Council as to the sharing of equipment, and dates must be arranged which will not conflict with each other. What preference is necessary should be given to the Boy Scout Troop. Rovers should be independent, and Senior Scouts on the way to independence, being encouraged to obtain light-weight equipment of their own.

(iii) Camping must not interfere with any boy's religious obligations, especially at week-ends. I have already emphasised this on page 112.

(iv) The camp programme must include training. There is no excuse for merely lazing at a week-end camp, or for using the summer camp as an easy means of lounging around the nearest seaside holiday resort.

(v) A high standard must be aimed at from the first, and the boys will respond. Our reputation for camping is, on the whole, good, and we must camp better than other people. This applies also to behaviour and dress of Scouts outside camp bounds.

(vi) The rules as to permits and safety must be strictly observed. These will be dealt with under separate headings below.

These six points are fundamental, and apply equally to

the long summer camp, the week-end camp, the trek and the hike.

The G.S.M. at camp

While the G.S.M.'s main responsibility is to supervise the arrangements before camp, the amount of supervision depending upon the experience of the Scouter who will be in charge, he will feel it his pleasant duty to visit as many camps as he can, and particularly the summer camp. But he will be wise to regard himself as a " paying guest," and not to interfere with the arrangements of the Scouter in charge unless he is asked to. But any offer to undertake a dull or dirty job will no doubt be heartily welcomed.

Early preparations

The ideal is for every Group to have its own private week-end site, which a landowner or farmer will let the Scouts use whenever they want to. He will perhaps allow them to leave some of their gear in a shed or barn. Scouters in the big towns will smile wryly at this, but it is surprising what can still be found if you search. There are, however, I.H.Q. and County (and in some cases District) sites near most of the big cities, and these have three special advantages, in that two or more boys can go there on their own, that inexperienced Troops can learn much from others camping there, and that lots of other Scouts—perhaps from other Counties and even Countries—can be met there. Scouters should find out in advance the arrangements for obtaining permission to camp, and what special regulations for camping have been found necessary (*e.g.* at Gilwell Park, owing to the soil, grease-pits are not dug). The boys should be told about these things before they go to such camps.

You need to start early to find a suitable site for the summer camp, or to lay plans for an expedition for seniors. Perhaps the G.S.M. can help there. He may have more time to look round; he may even have a car in which he can transport the Scouter. The camping textbooks mentioned below deal fully with the selection of sites, and it is only necessary to say here that some people should study them more carefully! Seaside sites are notoriously poor and to be avoided, and there are plenty of good inland sites where bathing can be obtained and the site is free. District Commissioners of rural areas are kind in supplying information about sites known to them, but they appreciate plenty of notice and the courtesy of a stamped addressed envelope for reply.

I.H.Q. issues to District Commissioners a list of unsuitable camp sites. These may be due to bad physical conditions or to being over-camped by other organisations or civilian camps. Before settling on any site, the G.S.M. should ask his own District Commissioner whether it is on the banned list.

Technical details of camping and hiking are outside the scope of this book. The official textbooks are "Standing Camps," "Scout Camps," and "Camping Standards."

The Camping Standards Certificate should, however, be mentioned. This has been found to be a definite encouragement to the boys to camp well. It is obtainable from I.H.Q. by the District Commissioner. The Group which wishes to use one asks for it when applying for permission to camp on form P.C. (see below), gets each Scout in camp to sign it, and displays it on the notice-board in camp. The visiting D.C. is asked to sign it after his inspection, and it becomes a Troop trophy, to be framed and exhibited in the headquarters.

Permission to camp

"No *Scouts* may camp without the previous permission of their District Commissioner" (P.O.R. 332 (i)). Few will deny that this is a reasonable precaution, in view of our responsibilities to parents and the general public.

The procedure is simple enough, but is worth stressing here because it is sometimes neglected, and Commissioners are justifiably annoyed if they find a camp in their district of which they have had no notice—especially if it is a bad one. Under P.O.R. 333, at least 21 days' notice of a summer camp, or 14 days' notice of any other camp, must be given on form P.C. by the Scouter in charge to his District Commissioner. When the Commissioner is satisfied, he signs the form and sends it on to the Secretary of the County in which the camp is to be held, and the Secretary in turn passes it to the District Commissioner of the camping area.

The G.S.M. also signs the form P.C., thus accepting on behalf of the Group responsibility for keeping the rules, and particularly those which relate to the safety of boys in boating and bathing. These will be mentioned later in this chapter. The form also asks for a map reference of the camp site, so that the local Commissioner will be able to find the camp. Unfortunately, many Scouters enter only a vague description such as " a field down the lane opposite the Church." By the time the Commissioner finds that the camp is actually not down that lane, but another one, he is not in the right mood for inspection. There are so many camps at the peak period in the popular camping areas that it is imperative that the description should be detailed and accurate, by reference to a good map.

The Group that makes its summer camp preparations well in advance will help everyone concerned if the P.C. form is sent on its journey as early as possible, and much earlier than the minimum of 21 days before the camp is due to start.

The special provisions for a Cub camp are dealt with below; a separate form (P.C. Cubs) is provided.

It is recognised that week-end camps and short hikes are often arranged at the last moment. Wherever possible, the P.C. procedure should be followed (P.O.R. 334), approximate dates being given. Where a Group has access to a site which it will use frequently during the season, one general notice at the beginning of the season will be sufficient.

Where time does not allow for the use of form P.C., the home District Commissioner may give permission to the G.S.M., at the beginning of the camping season and for not more than one year at a time, to use the special permit cards provided by I.H.Q. (P.O.R. 336-337). There are two of these cards—one for short Patrol camps and the other for hikes for Senior Scouts and Rovers. These cards are a great convenience, but the District Commissioner will not issue them automatically, and it is up to the Group to satisfy him that the boys who will use them can be relied on as properly trained. And it is up to the G.S.M. to see that they are only issued to fully reliable boys. Even where the cards are used, a postcard to the Commissioner of the camping or hiking area will be appreciated as a courtesy, if time permits.

Visits abroad

Even greater care must be taken if it is proposed to take Scouts abroad. As they will be entering the territory of the Scouts of another nation, the permission of Imperial Headquarters must first be obtained (P.O.R. 338). Sanction will not be given to Cubs to camp abroad, or indeed to travel abroad except in very unusual circumstances. But I am sure that no one in his right mind would want to take Cubs abroad; he wouldn't be in his right mind when he got back!

Plans for going abroad should start at least a year ahead, and it is wise to consult the District Commissioner before any plans are published to parents or boys. He will only give consent to visits by experienced and reliable people, and the G.S.M. had better ascertain, right at the start, whether his Scouters are regarded in that light by the Commissioner. When he has been squared, preliminary plans can be made and the camp bank can be opened. At that stage, get into touch with the International Department at I.H.Q. (or the Overseas Department, if you are going to a British possession). They will send you application forms and help you with general advice, but they are not travel agents and the Group must make its own arrangements. When I.H.Q. is satisfied as to the plans (including the plans for financing the visit), they will issue the International

Letter of Introduction, without which no journey abroad involving contacts with other Scouts can be permitted, and no facilities will be afforded by the Scout authorities of the foreign country.

If the Group would like advice from the Scout Headquarters of another country as to a good camp site or good hiking country, it must apply to I.H.Q. by 31st March.

It is unwise to include in your plans Scouts under 14. They are not old enough to get full value out of the trip, and I.H.Q. will not easily be persuaded to let them go. Speaking from personal experience of many years ago, I can testify that the younger boys were bored and tired by the sightseeing that the older ones wanted to do in Paris, and would have been much happier playing cricket on a bumpy pitch in a field at home.

Glad Bincham's book, "Camping Abroad," will amply repay the money you spend on it. There is another little book called "Scout Vocabularies," giving Scout terms in various languages. But it is to be hoped that boys who are going abroad will take the trouble to learn a bit more of the language of the country.

Guests from abroad

Many Groups have established links with Scout Troops from other nations, through contacts made at Jamborees or other visits, or through letters exchanged under the Link-up and Pen-pal schemes (see page 193). To invite a foreign Troop, or a Patrol, to join your Group in camp in this country is about the best way of making international friendships. The International Department at I.H.Q. get a number of enquiries from abroad as to the possibility of such visits, and will be glad to hear from any reliable Group who would like to entertain such guests. If you want to issue an invitation direct to any foreign Scouts you know, please do it through your own Commissioner and I.H.Q. It will be wise to remind your guests that they must bring with them their own International Letter of Introduction.

Hitch-hiking

This practice is so commonly followed by the general public, and receives so much attention in the papers, that it is not surprising that Senior Scouts and Rovers are tempted to follow it themselves. But it has been clearly stated by the Chief Scout that it is not good Scouting, and the following policy, which I quote in full, has been laid down: —

"The Chief Scout and the Committee of the Council have considered most carefully the practice of planning hikes and other journeys on the assumption that free travel will be possible by begging lifts on the roads (commonly known as 'hitch-hiking'). They are of the opinion that a false glamour has been attached to this method of travel, which really requires less initiative and planning than an adventurous hike or camp; that, by causing annoyance to the public, it may well bring the Movement into disrepute; and that it is an undesirable method for *Scouts,* who should aim at being self-reliant and self-supporting.

"It has been decided, therefore, that *Scouts* may only ask for lifts in an emergency, and Commissioners are requested to make this clear to those who are planning journeys in this country or abroad."

To which I would add three brief comments: —

(i) a Scout obeys orders;

(ii) it is all a question of training in the Group, so that boys understand the reasons for the order;

(iii) going abroad does not exempt a Scout from obeying the order. Indeed, it is from the Continent that the most bitter complaints have been received about hitch-hiking.

Women at Scout camps

(This section does not refer to women at Cub camps. These are dealt with in the next section.)

In exceptional circumstances, a warrant as Scoutmaster

of a Boy Scout Troop is issued to a woman. Experience has shown that such a woman has the qualities necessary to run a Scout camp, but she must observe the following precautions: —

(i) her own camp must be quite separate from that of the Scouts;

(ii) she must avoid embarrassing the boys by being present at inopportune moments;

(iii) she will need a male A.S.M. to be in charge at night;

(iv) she must do nothing to interfere with the Patrol Leaders' responsibilities.

A much more common difficulty is that of the married man who has to choose between running his Troop camp and taking his wife for a holiday. All the G.S.M.'s wisdom of advice may be necessary in dealing with such a case. Can the G.S.M. himself take the camp? Are any of the A.S.M.s of sufficient experience to take charge? They may well be capable, but not have had the chance of showing it. Can the Troop combine with another Troop? If none of those questions can be answered in the affirmative, can the married Scoutmaster take his wife with him, if she is prepared to go? Well, of course, it depends upon the kind of wife! She may be prepared, or indeed desire, to camp, or to secure accommodation nearby. The problem can only be solved by common sense and human sympathy, and those are qualities which all G.S.M.s are expected to possess. The following points may be suggested for his guidance: —

(i) the summer camp is the climax of the year's work, and must be held if humanly possible;

(ii) it must be a Scout camp and not a holiday lounge;

(iii) how much experience have the Patrols had in looking after themselves in camp?

(iv) if they will need much supervision, will there be a capable A.S.M. or A.S.M.s to provide it, or will the Scoutmaster feel he must be constantly on the spot?

(v) will the Scoutmaster be able to be away from camp with his wife for some time every day?

(vi) can it be guaranteed that the wife (especially if she is camping)—

(*a*) has a separate camp with her husband away from the boys;

(*b*) will not do any of the Patrol Leaders' jobs, such as cooking for them;

(*c*) will not get in the way?

The G.S.M. would do well to consult his District Commissioner at an early stage if he wishes to recommend that the Scoutmaster's wife should go to camp with him, for the Commissioner will need to be satisfied as to the arrangements before he signs the form P.C.

Boating and Bathing

The Scouter in charge of a camp takes over the parents' responsibilities for the safety of the boys while under his care, and he signs a declaration on form P.C. that if boating or bathing are to be undertaken, the rules in P.O.R. will be strictly obeyed. There are, fortunately, very few fatal accidents in comparison with the number of Scout camps, but every year there are one or two in which blame attaches to the Scouter in charge. His feelings in such a terrible case may be imagined, but it is difficult to sympathise with him if the accident could have been avoided by following the rules. As the G.S.M. has also signed the undertaking on form P.C., he often has to share in the blame.

The only course is to play safe, to be thoroughly acquainted with the rules in P.O.R. 146, 327 and 328, and to follow them in detail. I do not propose to go through them here, but will make a few comments.

BOATING (P.O.R. 146 and 327)

Safety precautions must be taken by all Troops proposing to use boats at any time. Even in inland waters, the precautions must be those which a prudent parent would take, but on open or tidal waters it is necessary to have far more stringent rules, and anyone in charge of a boat must hold a Charge Certificate. This is issued in your home District, and the G.S.M. who does not know about these things should consult his Commissioner at a very early stage, as it may not be easy to arrange for its issue in an inland County which has little water used by Sea Scouts. Even if you manage to secure a Charge Certificate, it is necessary to ascertain what local Sea Scout rules apply to the water you want to use and the kind of activity you want to follow. I think that by the time the G.S.M. of a non-Sea Scout Group has studied the rules, he will decide against any Scout boating on open or tidal waters. I certainly should. But I assume you can still arrange for a trip on the local " Saucy Sue " under the charge of the Ancient Mariner.

BATHING (P.O.R. 328)

The first thing is to find out where the boys will be bathing. Even in a properly supervised swimming-bath, or where the Scouter in charge has previously made sure that the whole of the water is shallow, and that there is no possible danger, accidents can happen, such as cramp or a heart-attack, and there should therefore be adult supervision.

In all other cases, it is necessary to seek local advice and follow it. The Scouter in charge of the party, or some responsible adult appointed by him for the purpose, must personally supervise the bathing. All reasonable precautions must be taken, including the provision of a life-line and a picket of two good swimmers.

But, I repeat, don't rely on these brief comments. Go

through the rules in detail and make sure that every point is covered.

IT IS BETTER TO BE SAFE THAN SORRY.

Cub Camps and Pack Holidays

While camping—by which I mean looking after yourself in the open air, doing your cooking, and sleeping in a tent —is essential to the proper training of a Scout, it forms no part of the training of a Cub. Whatever a Pack does by way of a summer holiday, it does not go camping in the Scout sense of the word. Nor does the Group allow its Cubs to camp with its Scouts (P.O.R. 332(ii)), except with the specific consent of the District Commissioner, and then only in exceptional circumstances. The G.S.M. and the Group Council should record their decision to have nothing to do with mixed camping.

Shall the Pack, then, go away on its own for a holiday? The G.S.M. and the Cub Scouters should have a clear understanding of the rules on this subject, not only because of the tender age of the Cubs but also because of the strain on the Cub Scouters. The rules offer two alternatives—a Pack holiday and a Cub camp—but there is no pressing need to do either. It is only the minority of Packs that spend a night or nights away. Day outings are the general custom.

If your Pack is in a crowded city area, and it seems unlikely that the Cubs will get a holiday in the country, your Cub Scouters may feel that they must do something about it. If so, preference should certainly be given to a Pack holiday rather than a camp.

PACK HOLIDAY (P.O.R. 341)

The Cubs must sleep indoors in a suitable building such as a Group headquarters, Church hall or school. Barns are not recommended. Water supply, cooking facilities and sanitation must be available under cover, in the building or immediately adjacent to it. Lots of adult help is needed. The rule lays down a minimum of two warranted Scouters (one of whom must be a Cub Scouter of experience), and at least one adult for every six Cubs present. If these conditions are fulfilled, all the Cubs can be taken.

The District Commissioner will be sticky about giving permission, and the G.S.M. will need to satisfy him that the leadership and accommodation are first rate.

CUB CAMP (P.O.R. 341A)

This is not an imitation of a Scout camp. It is a holiday in the country, where the Cubs sleep under canvas. But sleeping in tents, away from parents, is considered too much for the younger Cubs, so the rule lays down that no Cub under $9\frac{1}{2}$ may be taken unless the District Commissioner gives his special permission. The normal exception is the younger brother of an older Cub where the parents want to go away at the same time.

In addition to the tents for sleeping, there must be some form of clean, permanent shelter available for bad weather, or in the last resort a weatherproof marquee. The number of staff must be at least as many as for a Pack holiday, and with a good deal more experience of looking after small boys in the open.

I should not dream of allowing any Cub Scouter to be in charge of a Cub camp unless he or she had gained experience by attending a camp run by an experienced Old Wolf. If need be, the G.S.M. must be quite firm on that point. In any case, the District Commissioner must be consulted very early on, for the rule provides that "a Scouter who has not previously been in charge of a Cub camp or whose camp has been the subject of an unsatisfactory report must obtain the preliminary permission of the D.C. at least three months before the proposed date of the camp and before any intimation of the camp has been given to either the Cubs or parents."

The "permission to camp" form, either for a Pack holiday or a camp, is P.C. (Cubs). No one should make plans for either without having read the standard book, "Pack Holidays and Cub Camping."

Having read it, you will, I rather hope, abandon the project.

Camp Reports

When any members of the Group are camping outside their own District, they come under the jurisdiction of the District Commissioner for the District in which their camp lies (P.O.R. 333). If he finds them camping in a completely unsuitable place, he has authority to tell them to move, and may be able to suggest a better site. If he finds them behaving in an un-Scoutlike way, to the detriment of Scouting locally, he can order them to pack up and go home. This should be clearly understood by both Scouters and boys before they go to camp. Fortunately, Scout standards are fairly high, and such drastic steps are rarely necessary.

But the District Commissioner for the camping area will try to visit the camps in his District wherever possible or send a deputy to do so. He will then return the form P.C. to the home District with a report. He will usually endeavour to make his inspection a pleasant and friendly one, and the good Scouter will appreciate any suggestions for improvement that may be made. But if an unsatisfactory report is made, the home D.C. will want to discuss it with the G.S.M. in order to ensure a better camp next year. In really bad cases, payment may have to be made for damage done locally, or disciplinary action may have to be taken against a Scouter. For the good reputation of Scouting, prompt and decisive action is necessary.

Exemption from control of camping

A leaflet explaining the law on this subject can be obtained from I.H.Q. The position can be summarised here by saying that a landowner who allows Scouts to camp on his land for any period, with or without payment, can be assured that—

(i) he is not breaking the law,

(ii) no previous consent of any authority has to be obtained,

(iii) the result will not be a claim by any local authority for some extra payment.

Use of Lorries

It is the most convenient and the least expensive way of getting Scouts and their equipment to camp to hire a lorry, but this raises some legal difficulties, which are explained in a leaflet obtainable from I.H.Q. It is too long to repeat it all here, but the G.S.M. should realise that the lorry-owner or driver may make himself liable to penalties, unless he has a licence to convey passengers in a commercial vehicle, and should make sure that all the necessary formalities, particularly as regards insurance, have been complied with.

Railway Travel

By arrangement with the British Railways Executive, *Scouts* can travel to and from camps and rallies in Great Britain at reduced rates, and railway ticket vouchers (form R.V.) can be obtained from Local Association Secretaries. The voucher must be presented at the time of booking the tickets; if not, ordinary fares will be charged.

The railways are willing to accept all camp equipment for conveyance in advance at the same charge as when accompanied by the passengers. Normally, this means free conveyance to the station nearest the site, but a charge is made for collection and delivery, if it suits the Troop to have the equipment collected from their headquarters and delivered to an agreed place near the site. Trek-carts, if taken to pieces and carried in the guard's van of the train conveying the party to camp, are carried free of charge.

Youth Hostels

The Youth Hostels Association, Welwyn Garden City, Herts (in Scotland, the Scottish Youth Hostels Association, 7 Bruntsfield Crescent, Edinburgh 10), is anxious to help Scouting whenever possible. They run hostels in most parts of Great Britain, and are affiliated to similar societies in many countries in Western Europe.

Senior Scouts and Rovers will find the hostels most useful for winter activities, although in summer their Scout training will incline them to camp and cook for themselves. The hardy ones who prefer a tent, even in the snow, will find that many hostels have patches of ground on which tents can be pitched. But there is no great attraction in sitting in a tent in semi-darkness from teatime to bedtime, and the hostels provide not only shelter but also the company of young people of all sorts. Membership is quite cheap.

Except during peak holiday periods and week-ends, the hostels can be booked for parties of boys from 9 to 16 years old, and are ideal for Cub Pack holidays. The only condition is that at least one adult to every ten boys must be a member of Y.H.A. To ensure accommodation, arrangements should be made well in advance.

CHAPTER 14

OLD SCOUTS

EVER since 1908, thousands of Scouts have left the Movement as they grew up, and many of them were most unwilling to go. Though they did not feel cut out to be Scouters, they knew that the Scout Promise and Law would continue to be their guides to conduct, and that it would help them to keep their Promise if they were still connected with Scouting in some way. It was inevitable that there should have been a demand for some form of Old Scout organisation almost from the beginning. The first Old Scouts Association of which I have heard was founded in 1912.

Such Associations were almost invariably connected with one Scout Troop, well established and blessed with a Scoutmaster to whom hundreds of Old Scouts looked back with respect and affection. But until 1947 there was little or nothing for the man whose Group had ceased to exist, or who had moved away from his original home and lost touch with it.

It was high time that something was attempted on a wider basis, and in 1947 the B.-P. Guild of Old Scouts was founded, at first under the general direction of Scout Headquarters, but with the avowed intention of becoming an independent body as soon as it was strong enough to stand by itself. This happened in October, 1950. But although the Guild is now responsible for its own affairs, it has always been the desire of both bodies that there should be the closest liaison between the Boy Scouts Association and the B.-P. Guild at all levels.

It is estimated that between two and three million men

and women have at some time been members of the Scout Movement in this country. Although some of these were unlucky enough to be in a dud Troop and may not look back to their Scouting with any pleasure, there are many hundreds of thousands whose experience was more fortunate, who remember their days in Troop or Pack with gratitude, and who still cherish the inspiration of the Law and Promise. Such people should be members of the B.-P. Guild, and it is to the obvious benefit of the community and of the Scout Movement that they should be brought into it.

Every well-established Group should have its own Branch of the Guild, run by its own Committee and Officers in close liaison with the G.S.M. It is a valuable source of strength to the Group, and a good example to the *Scouts* of to-day of the continuing influence of the Scout spirit among adults.

The objects of the Guild are wide enough to cover everybody. They are—

(1) to keep alive among the members the spirit of the Scout Promise and Law,

(2) to carry that spirit into the communities in which they live and work,

(3) to give support to the Scout Movement, so far as their other responsibilities will allow.

The order is important. It is not the *prime* object of the Guild to provide more Scouters, or even to help the Scout Movement, but to help Old Scouts themselves and the community. Many who have passed through the Scout Movement have established themselves in successful careers and in innumerable forms of public service, and are too busy to give time to Scouting. They would not become members of the Guild if they felt that service to Scouting was demanded of them. But they are wanted as members, and can indeed be most useful to Scouting in their own way. How frequently do we find, when we ask a stranger for advice, that he is willing to go out of his way to give it—because he was a Scout once.

But there are many others who are not too busy to help Scouting directly. They may not have time, ability or inclination to be Scouters, but there are many other ways in which their help can be invaluable, as members of Group Committees, Instructors or Examiners, for example. In many places, teams of Old Scouts have taken over the work of running District sports events or swimming galas. One Cub Pack I know is lucky enough to have pairs of Old Scouts taking duty, for a day at a time, at their Pack holiday. Old Scouts in office or factory can, by their example and by wearing their badge, be a wonderful help to a Scout who has just taken up his first job and may be wondering whether the Scout Law is one of those things which you give up when you leave school. To put it at the lowest, a Scout Group can get far more help from its Old Scout Branch than it is likely to be able to give.

But when a Branch is being formed, the Scouters of the Group can be of the greatest help, and the Guild will be grateful for it. They are the people who will know where the old Scouts are to be found, and which of them are likely to be useful Officers or Committee members of the new Branch, and it may be by their persuasion that these people are brought in.

Once the Branch is formed, the Old Scouts will run it, but liaison must continue. Members of the Group should be on the Committee of the Old Scout Branch, and Old Scouts on the Group Committee. The Group should welcome Old Scouts at their social functions, and keep them in touch with what is going on. In particular, the Scouters of the sections should not be backward in telling the Old Scout Committee what help they need.

Above all, the B.-P. Guild must look to the Scout Movement for recruits, as boys grow too old to be Scouts and come to the time when they must leave. Far too many are allowed to drift away without hearing anything about the Guild. Group Scouters should always remember that, even if their Group has not been able to start a Branch of the Guild, there are other Branches locally, either for the District as a whole, or in a large factory or in another Group. It is up to the G.S.M. to see that information is available, and that names and addresses are passed to the Guild Secretary.

Unfortunately, the majority of boys leave Scouting before they are old enough to become members of the Guild, the minimum age for which is 18, and there may be a long gap, during which the boy may be lost sight of. I have not yet heard of any successful way of getting over this difficulty. The only suggestion I can make is that Scouters should give to the Guild Secretary the names, addresses and ages of the boys concerned at the time they leave the Group, and leave it to the Guild Secretary to approach the ex-Scout when he becomes 18.

Old Scouts and Rovers

The Group Council should be clear in their minds as to the relationship between Rovers and Old Scouts, of which something has already been said on page 155.

Where there is no Rover Crew, as is the case in the majority of Groups, no difficulty arises. But where there is a Crew, it is most important to avoid overlapping, and the ill-feeling that comes from "body-snatching." The distinction is really obvious, for the Rover Crew should be an active body of young men who are still engaged in

Scout activities and joint training, whereas the Old Scout Branch consists of a body of men of very diverse interests and ages, who are bound together not so much by the activities they pursue in common as by their common adherence to the Scout Law and Promise. But if the Rover Crew is really an Old Scout Branch which dresses up in uniform on occasions, there is bound to be confusion. The remedy is with the Rover Crew!

CHAPTER 15

PUBLIC RELATIONS

"PUBLIC relations," for the purpose of this chapter, means two things. First, telling the local world what the Group is doing. Second, being in friendly touch with our neighbours.

For this, the G.S.M. is mainly responsible, as head of the Group, but he will not be very successful unless every member of the Group, down to the youngest Cub, realises that he has a part to play and is prepared to play it. It has often been said that the best advertisement for Scouting is a smart *Scout* and a well-run Group.

Example

Neighbours, teachers, other boys at school, employers and fellow-employees, all judge the Scout Movement by the *Scouts* they know locally. Every day of their lives, all our *Scouts* are living advertisements for Scouting, and the advertisement may be attractive or repulsive. If the teaching of the Scout Law and Promise is sound, its members will attract the public by their cheerfulness, their keenness at school or at work, and by their good manners.

Appearance

Every Group should make constant use of that valuable pamphlet, "Smartness in Scouting." Here is one paragraph from it: "Scouting is judged mainly by what is seen in public. It is therefore the duty of every Scout, whether he be man or boy, to see to it that his personal appearance, bearing and behaviour always reflect credit on the Movement." And in the Foreword, the Chief Scout says: "In spite of our efforts, we still find Scouts and Scouters sloppy and badly turned out on big occasions. . . . A proper bearing and smart pace give us a pride in ourselves which we can never experience otherwise. It is a habit which is just as easy to acquire as sloppiness, and what a difference it makes to our outlook on life, and the opinion of other people about us! Go to it, Scouters, make those inspections real inspections: only the best is good enough."

No wonder that the Chief Scout wrote as he did, for when he was received by His late Majesty King George VI on his appointment, the King drew his attention to the fact that *Scouts* seldom gave an appearance of smartness, especially in the mass.

See that your Group determines to set a high standard, and that the example is set by the Scouters. Smartness of uniform will help a great deal—with hat brims pressed, scarves ironed, and badges neatly sewn on in the right place.

We who live in London see many *Scouts* who visit I.H.Q. Many of them make us feel very proud of Scouting, but we get depressed sometimes when we are invaded by a horde of scruffy-looking creatures, rushing all over the place and shouting at the tops of their voices. One look at the Scouter usually explains everything!

Discipline

I know that the best discipline is that which comes from within, and arises from the boys' habit of observing the Scout Law. All the same, a bit of outward discipline helps, and boys like it. As the Chief Scout wrote, in the passages quoted above, " make those inspections real inspections," with the Patrol Leader calling his Patrol to the alert. The use of the salute can be an aid to discipline without losing its meaning as a form of greeting; I believe in a Scout saluting his Scoutmaster (and being saluted in return) when he arrives for a Troop meeting.

Troops vary greatly in the way in which Scouts address their Scouters. Some have always used the term " Sir, and there is much to be said for it, but " Skip " seems to work quite well. There is much less to be said for using Christian names, and nothing to be said for derogatory nicknames. The best Scoutmaster I ever knew was invariably called " Charlie," but he was an exceptional man and could get away with it. The ordinary Scouter, who is not exceptional, would do well to bar the use of his Christian name.

As to drill, I believe we have reached a balanced view about it. Too much drill destroys individuality, as B.-P. said even in his Army days, but the right quantity of it is needed to enable Troops (and indeed Packs) to move in orderly fashion in public. As B.-P. said: " Drill is not the prerogative of the Army—or of the Navy or the Air Force, for that matter. It is used in different forms of civil life and in industry so that a man may learn to do things in the right way in the right order." Consult the pamphlet " Smartness in Scouting."

Ceremonies

Ceremonies are short and simple in Scouting, and in consequence all the easier to carry out well. They make a deep impression on their central figures, whether at a " going-up " ceremony or at an investiture, as well as upon any visitors such as parents who are invited to be present. Why, then, are our ceremonies so often slipshod and undignified? The reason may be lack of preparation or lack of discipline, which are within the power of any Group to prevent.

In particular, I would beg the Scoutmaster or Cubmaster who is conducting a ceremony to be sure of his words, to take trouble in preparation and, in case of nervousness which may afflict anyone, to have the words of the Promise written in large capital letters on a postcard lying on the table in front of him. As I have quoted in another connection, " it is better to be safe than sorry."

Publicity

Some Scouters dislike the sound of the word " publicity," perhaps because they have had experience of undesirable forms of it in other connections. But a Scout Group cannot avoid some publicity, and it may as well be good. It will have to appear in public from time to time, and it will want to get the public to its annual show and its other money-raising events.

Fortunately, I.H.Q. has published a valuable book, named " Public Occasions," in which a number of experienced people have given much wise advice as to organising every type of public occasion. I commend it to all G.S.M.s, and pass on to other types of publicity.

The Press

Space is hard to obtain in the national Press, but there are hundreds of local papers, all anxious to publish news which will interest their public. It may be that your Local Association has a Press Representative, from whom you can get advice as to the kind of news the local paper takes, and how it should be presented. If not, see if one of your Group Committee members cannot get you an introduction to the Editor or one of the journalists, who will usually be quite ready to give you the same type of advice. He'll probably turn out to have been a Scout himself!

The point is that Scout news should appear in the paper, and news about your Group can best come from the Group itself. The kind of news which is wanted is not a long article on " The Scout Spirit," but Tom Jones's First Class badge or the Seniors who are going to cycle across Europe to Austria, together with their names and addresses.

Moreover, invite the Press to your annual show.

Annual Report

I feel that it should be the ambition of every Group to publish an annual report. It need not be elaborate; a duplicated sheet is good enough for a small Group in its early years. But the large, well-established Group will find it worth while to have its report printed, and circulated to Group Committee members, subscribers, and to all parents. Much of it will be news to many parents, who get little enough from the boys themselves.

Annual Meeting

I like the idea of an annual meeting for everyone who is concerned as an adult in the life of the Group. Scouts and Cubs are not admitted, but Patrol Leaders, Senior Scouts and Rovers should be there on duty. It need not cost the Group much, for many parents and members of the Committee will supply the refreshments without which such a meeting would be but dust and ashes. Send out nice invitation cards to all parents and supporters, Old Scouts, members of Committees, Scouters, and in the case of a Church-sponsored Group, the Sponsoring Authority, the Chaplain, and any member of the congregation who has helped or shown interest. And don't forget the District Commissioner and his Assistants, and the Chairman, Secretary and Treasurer of the Local Association. This is your opportunity to tell the folk what has been done during the year, and to give them copies of your annual report, which will enable you to cut down the talking. A display of photographs, old and new, on the walls will always be popular. Give an opportunity for questions. Finish off with something special such as a talk by a Scouter from another country, or a film, or a short demonstration by your Troop or a Patrol. Friendliness and informality will make the annual meeting into a happy family reunion.

Notice Board

A notice board outside your headquarters is good publicity only if it is well maintained, kept in good repair and furnished with up-to-date information. That sounds elementary, doesn't it? But look around at local notice boards and see if the warning is not needed. The name and address of the G.S.M. should appear clearly, so that people who call at the H.Q. and find it closed know where to go for information.

Group Magazine

The whole country is strewn with the corpses of Group magazines which have been brought to birth with great labour, but have died of starvation after a few months of life. So don't start one unless you can see your way to keep it going. Mind you, they are excellent things, but they do seem fantastically difficult to keep alive.

But a more modest endeavour such as a quarterly news-sheet can be run without too much trouble, and has among other values the great advantage of enabling you to keep in touch with chaps who are doing their National Service or who are at sea or doing other work which takes them from home.

Recruiting Campaigns are seldom worth while for attracting either boys or adults. If yours is a good Group, you have probably got a waiting-list already. If it isn't, it isn't quite honest to campaign for recruits. Both boys and adults are attracted by personal contact rather than by general invitations to roll up.

Other relationships

Besides telling the world what we are doing, we want to be on friendly terms with our neighbours. And who are our neighbours?

May I put in a plea for the people who live near our headquarters? I fear that some of them suffer severely and, on the whole, patiently. Noise they must expect, but not uncontrolled noise. At least Scouters can see that Cubs and Scouts go home promptly when meetings are over, and with no more than the usual babble.

An occasional call by one of the Scouters on these neighbours would be an act of courtesy, and it might be appreciated if he enquired whether the *Scouts* could help in any way in the house or garden.

Parents have been mentioned many times already. I will only repeat that for every reason of courtesy and expediency it is essential for the Scouters to be in close and friendly touch with all the parents, and the best form of contact is to see them in their homes.

Youth Organisations

Most Group Scouters are short of spare time, and have few opportunities of meeting leaders of other youth organisations. But at least they should know what other organisations exist in their neighbourhood, and should see that as Scouters they do nothing which may lead to ill-feeling or over-keen rivalry. There is plenty of room for all, and different boys prefer different methods. I am thinking specially of branches of the Boys' Brigade, Church Lads' Brigade, Boys' Clubs, Cadets, Red Cross and St. John Ambulance Cadets, and Young Farmers' Clubs.

We may lament it if a Scout leaves us to join one of these bodies, but the boy is free to choose, and generally speaking will remain a Scout if the Group is good enough to keep him. It is up to us as Scouters to make the Group good enough. But the Headquarters of all the organisations deprecate any deliberate attempt on the part of any leader to persuade a boy to transfer. Any such case which affects a Group should be reported to the District Commissioner (see pages 131-132).

Squabbles sometimes occur at Youth Parades as to which organisation takes precedence. It is to be hoped that Scouters never raise such points. What does it matter?

Opportunities may arise for an occasional joint activity with Senior Scouts and their opposite numbers in the Boys' Brigade or other unit—a social evening, perhaps, or a debate. Such an opportunity should not be neglected.

Girl Guides

It is the general policy of the Scout Movement that co-operation with the Girl Guides should be closer than that with any other youth organisation, because our aims and many of our methods are identical. This applies at all levels, but is specially necessary where a Church has a Guide Company as well as a Scout Group. Such co-operation is mainly at leader level, in order that policy may be the same as often as possible, but joint activities between boys and girls are not ruled out. They form the subject of P.O.R. 31-32.

Rule 31 says that, except as set out in Rule 32, *Scouts* and *Guides* should not be trained together. Rule 32 says: The following forms of joint training of *Scouts* and *Guides* may be encouraged when the circumstances are suitable; but competitions between *Scouts* and *Guides* are undesirable except as an occasional item in a social event.

Sub-para. (1) deals with the exceptional case of Cubs and Brownies in schools, or in other special circumstances, and does not concern the ordinary Group. Generally, they are kept apart, except for an occasional tea-and-games affair.

Sub-para. (2) limits the joint training of Scouts and Guides to specific subjects where special arrangements can be made, and to occasional joint recreation, subject to proper supervision and the approval of the respective Commissioners. Scouts under 15 are not usually very interested in the opposite sex.

Sub-para. (3) deals with co-operation between Rovers or Senior Scouts and Rangers, and this is often extremely successful as a means of training. In a Church-sponsored Group, for example, the " over-15s " and the Rangers can easily join in acts of service to the Church, and this can be arranged at Group level. Other forms of joint activity (of which many examples are given in the rule) may well be on a District basis with the approval of the respective Commissioners.

Sub-para. (4) is little known, and could perhaps be used more than it is. It permits the exchange of Scout and Guide training instructors for the teaching of subjects in which they are specially proficient. I have heard from time to time of a Guider being asked to teach Scouts how to cook, and of a Scouter being asked to teach Guides woodcraft. And a very good thing, too.

Mention has already been made of the great help which many Cub Packs receive from Rangers and Cadets who help as Cub Instructors and, when they are old enough, become A.C.M.s and C.M.s. They are very welcome, but we must restrain our eagerness to ask them until we have got the agreement of their Captain.

Adult Societies

There are many adult societies which urge many of their members to offer service to the community. Among them are the Y.M.C.A., the British Legion, Toc H, Rotary, the Round Table and the Women's Institutes. The District Commissioner is probably in touch with their local Headquarters with a view to getting help for Scouting. Groups should not be backward in making their needs known, and in opening their doors to visitors from such societies who may want to see how Scouting works.

Branches of Toc H, in particular, have been urged by their Headquarters to give as much help to Scouting as possible.

Local Authorities

Our main contacts with local authorities are probably at District or County level, but G.S.M.s should make it their business to find out what opportunities are available for their *Scouts*. Every now and then the Mayor asks whether the local Scouts can help him at some function, or take part in a Youth Parade. Groups are generally very good at responding to such requests, but might be stricter than they sometimes are in seeing that selected Scouts are smartly turned out and know what they are expected to do.

On the other hand, the local authority provides facilities for Scouts which are not always fully used. For example, the use of the public library (see "Libraries," pages 214-215), or special times at the swimming baths.

Probation Officers

The G.S.M. should certainly be in touch with the Probation Officer. Many of them will be found to be old Scouts, and anxious that some of the boys who have got into trouble should be taken into a Scout Troop. The influence of a good Troop with a live and adventurous programme has saved many such boys.

On the other hand, it may happen that one of your nice little Scouts gets into trouble, and it is you that may need the help of the Probation Officer. You will, I am sure, find him very sympathetic, and I know that Juvenile Court Magistrates are glad to have the witness of a Scouter, if one of his boys has to make an appearance before them.

Youth Employment Officers

It is the special job of the Youth Employment Officer to advise young people as to the work which will suit them best, and to place local opportunities before them. He will welcome being consulted by Scouters as to particular boys, and is usually in his office during one or more evenings in the week to meet people who cannot see him during the daytime (see page 146).

CHAPTER 16

THE DISTRICT COMMISSIONER AND THE LOCAL ASSOCIATION

UP to this point, we have been considering the Group as a self-contained unit. It is time to think of it now as part of a world-wide organisation, with a world membership of over five millions, and a national membership of half a million.

In this chapter, we shall deal in briefest outline with the local organisation of Scouting, and in the next with the national and international set-up.

From the beginning, the Scout Movement has followed the principle of decentralisation, as much authority as possible being delegated by the national body to the local representatives of Scouting. This makes it all the more important that Scouters should understand how the machine works, what their part in it is, and the necessity for complete loyalty, not only to Scout principles, but to those who are responsible for seeing that they are carried into effect.

At the top is the Chief Scout and the Council of the Boy Scouts Association, then come County Commissioners and County Scout Councils, then District Commissioners and Local Associations, then G.S.M.s and Groups.

The District is the area for which the District Commissioner is responsible. The area of the Local Association is usually the same, but in a few places there may be two or even more Local Associations in one District.

The District Commissioner

The District Commissioner is appointed by Imperial Headquarters on the advice of the County Commissioner.

His duties are set out under no less than eleven sub-heads in P.O.R. 125, but can be summarised briefly as follows. He is the representative of the Chief Scout, and responsible for the interpretation of Scout policy and rules, and for seeing that they are loyally followed by Scouters and *Scouts*. He is responsible for the welfare and progress of the Movement in his District, and for the training of Scouters and *Scouts*. In short, as the Chief's representative he is head of Scouting in the District, and accepted as such, not only by Scouters but by the community as a whole.

It is, perhaps, even more important that he should be not only the leader but the friend of all his Scouters, to whom they can and will go for advice and help, and who in his turn leaves them the maximum freedom to carry on their Groups.

In all this, he works in friendly co-operation with the Local Association, the duties of which are described below.

Assistant District Commissioners

The duties of a District Commissioner are so numerous that he cannot expect to carry them all out single-handed. To help him, he has a staff of Assistant Commissioners, whose number will vary widely according to the size of the District. An Assistant Commissioner may be appointed for general duties, acting as the Commissioner's deputy or assisting him for a specified part of the District, or for special duties, specialising in Cubs or Scouts or Senior Scouts, etc. His duties will be definied by the District Commissioner. Usually, the section leader in a Group looks to the specialist A.D.C. (*e.g.* for Cubs) for advice and help in regard to his section, while the G.S.M. looks to the D.C. But the wise D.C. takes an interest in each section alike, and avoids making compartments too watertight.

District Scouters

In some Districts, District Scouters are appointed (District Cubmaster, District Scoutmaster, etc.) in addition to, or instead of, Assistant Commissioners, by the D.C. and L.A. jointly, and their duties are such as the D.C. may allot to them.

The Local Association

Alongside the D.C. is the Local Association, in much the same relation to him as the Group Committee to the G.S.M. but with greater responsibility in certain directions. It is responsible for finance and publicity, for the supervision of Group finances, Group Committees, trusts for Group property, and for arranging examinations for proficiency badges and their issue. Jointly with the D.C., the L.A. is responsible for recommendations for Scouters' warrants, Group registrations, and certain other matters. These are more fully described in the pamphlet, "Local Associations."

The day-to-day work of the L.A. is carried out by an Executive Committee, on which Scouters and lay members should have equal representation.

There is no limit to the number of members of a Local Association. The more of the local community that can be roped in, the better. Usually, there are far too few. They consist of (1) certain ex-officio members, including all G.S.M.s and all section leaders who hold warrants in the area, (2) elected members, being any persons (including Scouters who do not qualify under (1)) elected at a meeting of the L.A., (3) associates, including parents of *Scouts,* Rovers and Old Scouts over 21, and supporters who pay a specified subscription, and (4) co-opted members, such as representatives of the Girl Guides, local education authorities and religious bodies (P.O.R. 136).

The Executive Committee will probably appoint sub-committees for specific purposes such as finance, warrants and badges.

It is the obvious duty of all Groups to give every support to the Local Association. They can encourage members of their Group Committees and parents to become members of the L.A. They should be punctilious in attending meetings, and their Scouters should, time permitting, take their full part in the work of Committees to which they are elected. At the same time, the Scouter's first duty is to his boys, and Local Associations should put severe limits on the number of meetings which a Scouter is expected to attend.

The Local Association may, by P.O.R. 186, require a small registration fee and/or an annual subscription from each Group. The practice varies widely from one place to another, but there is no good reason why a Group should not take its share of the expenses of the L.A., so long as the L.A. never forgets that its prime duty is to help the Groups, and not vice versa.

The job of the G.S.M.

The G.S.M. is the channel of communication between the Group and the D.C. and L.A. Notices will be sent to him, unless they are of purely sectional interest, and it is of the greatest importance that he should ensure that all the Scouters of the Group see them quickly. It is a great help to the L.A. Secretary if census returns, annual accounts and schedules of property (inventories) are sent in by the due dates.

In particular, through the Group Council, he must arouse and maintain an active interest in—

(i) opportunities for training, of whatever kind,

(ii) attendance at Scouters' meetings,

(iii) District events such as the sports meeting, swimming gala, conference, rally or camp.

It is not just a question of Scouters loyally supporting District activities, although that is important. It is even more important that both Scouters and *Scouts* should have every opportunity of meeting their brother Scouters and *Scouts* from other Groups, and of realising that they are not just members of the Umpteenth Group, but also part of a world-wide brotherhood. Isolationism has no place in Scouting.

It is a help if Districts fix the dates of events at least six months and preferably a year in advance, so that Groups can keep those dates free and avoid any unfortunate collision of events. And, as the main training of *Scouts* takes place within the Group, the wise District will avoid arranging too many District events.

To sum up, the keynotes of success in a District are—

(i) to put the interests of the boys first all the time,

(ii) to work as a team of friends with the D.C.,

(iii) when necessary, to accept the D.C.'s decision or that of the L.A. loyally, in the spirit of the Scout Law,

(iv) to look wide—beyond the Group, to the District, and through the District to the County and Imperial Headquarters.

CHAPTER 17

LOOKING WIDER

IT is to be feared that many *Scouts* go through Pack or Troop without realising that they are members of a world-wide brotherhood without equal in any other sphere. Even if, at his investiture, the boy is told that he is now a member of the world-wide brotherhood of Scouts, it will mean little, if his Cubmaster or Scoutmaster has not told him anything about it. It is so vague as to be meaningless.

It is the job of the G.S.M. to impress upon his section leaders that this is an essential part of their preparation of the boy for investiture. To do this, the Scouters will have to prepare themselves, not only to adopt the right attitude of " looking wide, and then looking wider still " (as B.-P. so often advised us), but also to know enough about the national and international aspects of Scouting to interest the boy.

Not only at his investiture, but throughout his Scout life the boy should be constantly reminded of these things. There are various ways in which this can be done. Some of the Senior Scouts may have camped abroad during the summer or even attended a World Jamboree. A Rover may have been to a World Rover Moot, or a Scouter to an Indaba. See that they tell the Cubs and Scouts about it, and show them their photographs. Even if no one from your Group has had such an experience recently, someone else in the District probably has, and will be glad to come and tell your Group about it.

Films of Jamborees and Moots can be hired from I.H.Q. Pictures and articles appear in " The Scouter " and " The Scout," and there is an international monthly magazine called "Jamboree," which is obtainable from the International Bureau and has an excellent pictorial section.

Many Scouters and Rovers, during their period of National Service, as well as Deep-Sea Rovers, have served overseas and have probably met *Scouts* or even helped to run them. People come home on leave from the Colonies and will be glad to tell your *Scouts* how people live in those remote places.

Two useful schemes are run by Imperial Headquarters. The first is the "Linking-up Scheme," under which a Group at home can be linked with a Group in the Empire or in a foreign country, or both. Particulars can be obtained from I.H.Q. The object of the scheme is that the two Groups should keep in touch with each other as much as possible, by letters, by exchange of interesting information and souvenirs of each other's country, and by interchange of personal and Troop visits and camps.

The second is the "Pen-Pal Scheme," for individual Scouts who like to have a permanent correspondent in another country. The appropriate form can be obtained from Imperial Headquarters, and when it is returned to them with the approval of the G.S.M., they do their best to find a Scout correspondent in the country chosen.

These schemes have proved to be valuable links in international Scout relationships, but should not be lightly undertaken. Great disappointment may be caused to a Group or a Scout abroad if correspondence, once started, is allowed to drop.

In making our plans, we should not overlook the countries of the Commonwealth and Empire. They are as keen as anyone to establish links of this kind, many of them think of this country as "home," and there is no barrier of language.

There is a danger that Scouters may fix their gaze on so wide a world horizon that they overlook the nearer features of the landscape. Our first and most important contacts are with the Scouts of our own District, County and country. The Group should play its full part in District affairs, and through the District realise the parts played in the scheme of things by the County and Imperial Headquarters.

It is worth remembering that, both historically and practically, the Scout District and Scout County are built up from the Groups, which are the basic units, but are strengthened by other supporters of Scouting.

The County

In normal circumstances, the Group has little direct contact with the affairs of the Scout County, which is in the charge of the County Commissioner and the County Scout Council. But the County authorities arrange some events for the benefit of Scouters and *Scouts,* and the G.S.M. should see that members of the Group take part in them.

The Camp Chief at Gilwell Park is responsible to I.H.Q. for the training of Scouters, but each County has its own Training Team, who arrange similar Wood Badge courses locally, either on their own or in conjunction with neighbouring Counties. While it is a natural ambition of most Scouters to take their Wood Badge course at Gilwell Park itself, there is not room for all, and many cannot afford the time to take a continuous course there. So the County Wood Badge courses (some of which are run at week-ends) are very necessary, and the G.S.M. should give them every support. Preliminary courses are not run at Gilwell Park, and are the sole responsibility of the County Training Team.

Other events which may be arranged by the County, annually or at longer intervals, are camping competitions, Senior Scout or Rover hikes, Scouters' conferences, and rallies, especially rallies to meet the Chief Scout, who naturally cannot manage visits to each of the 1,000 Districts in the country. These merit the support of all Groups, for they are a valuable factor in the education of *Scouts* and Scouters alike.

The G.S.M. may be called upon to take part in the work of the County Scout Council, for each Local Association elects three representatives to it, and one of them must be a Scouter. If he finds himself elected as a member, he must remember that he is responsible, not only for considering County arrangements, but also for bringing back to his Local Association and Group any news or views of importance which he may have gained at the meeting.

It is unlikely that any serious dispute will occur between Group Scouters and the District Commissioner, but if unfortunately such a dispute should arise which the D.C. is unable to settle, P.O.R. 125 (3) provides that it must be referred to the County Commissioner for settlement.

Imperial Headquarters

A 64-page booklet, entitled "What I.H.Q. Does," gives a description of the varied activities of Imperial Headquarters, and the reader is referred to it for full information. I know of many Scouters who, after long service in the Movement, read it and confessed that they had no idea how many-sided is the work of I.H.Q. I can only touch briefly on a few points here.

I.H.Q. is responsible for the policy, development and welfare of Scouting in the United Kingdom and the Colonies, comprising about 600,000 *Scouts*, of whom half a million are in this country. There are over 50 Colonial Branches. The Dominions govern their own affairs, but keep in very close touch with I.H.Q.

The Boy Scouts Association was incorporated by Royal Charter in 1912. The Charter lays down that the Association shall be governed by a Council, of which the Chief

Scout is Chairman. But the general administration is carried out by the Committee of the Council, the members of which are elected by the Council and come up for re-election every three years, one-third retiring annually.

The Departments at I.H.Q. are administered, so far as matters of policy are concerned, by part-time Commissioners who give their services voluntarily, and whose activities are co-ordinated by the Chief Executive Commissioner. General administration is the province of the Administrative Secretary. The staff as a whole has a very wide experience of Scouting, not only here but overseas.

(Scotland has its own Headquarters and " Policy, Organisation and Rules," in order to deal with its special conditions, but works in close liaison with I.H.Q., and is represented on the Committee of the Council.)

Some of the Departments, such as that dealing with Grants, have already been mentioned in this book, and I will only add a few notes regarding other Departments which are of direct concern to Group Scouters.

The Scout Shop, with its branches, exists for service to the Scout Movement and has an extensive knowledge of *Scout* needs. The profits are entirely used for the benefit of the Movement, by helping to meet the administration expenses of I.H.Q. While we have no monopoly of the supply of *Scout* uniform and equipment, all Groups are urged to buy such things from the Scout Shops, as they can be sure of the quality and suitability of what is sold, and they are directly helping to ensure the financial stability of the Movement.

Gilwell Park is part of I.H.Q., and as already mentioned is responsible for the training of Scouters. The original training scheme, as laid down by the Founder himself in 1919, is still in operation, and has attracted Scouters from nearly all the countries of the world. Twice since B.-P.'s death, the International Conference has formally recognised

Gilwell Park as the international training centre, and its importance as a unifying factor in world Scouting is vital.

"*The Scouter*" and "*The Scout*" are the means by which I.H.Q., and particularly the Chief Scout, is able to keep in touch with Scouters and *Scouts*. They are, moreover, full of things which we ought to know and think about. Each Scouter should have his personal copy of "The Scouter." Rovers and Senior Scouts (at any rate those of 16 and over) will be interested in much of its contents, so there should be a copy or two for circulation. One copy at least should be kept reasonably untattered, so that it can be filed for future reference.

The Publications Board is I.H.Q.'s own publishing house, and shares with Messrs. Pearsons, and Brown, Son & Ferguson, the task of producing the books which the Movement needs.

The Legal Adviser not only looks after all the legal and parliamentary business of I.H.Q., but spends a considerable part of his time in more direct help to Districts and Groups, in such matters as Scouters in trouble, Trust Deeds, and general advice on legal and business matters.

The Overseas and International Departments have been mentioned several times already, in connection with the migration of *Scouts*, foreign visits, and so on. They are our liaison officers with the *Scouts* of other countries. The Overseas Department is directly responsible for Scouting in the Colonies. The International Department is our Foreign Office. It is not, as some Scouters seem to think, responsible for the supervision of Scouting all over the world. That is the task of the International Bureau, which we will consider below.

The Field Commissioners are employed and paid by I.H.Q., but their services are lent to areas consisting of two or more Counties. They work under the direction of the County Commissioners in the area to which they are allotted, and as they are constantly travelling in their areas, many Group Scouters will know them, and appreciate their advice and help.

B.-P.'s Room is on the first floor of the I.H.Q. offices and is open to visitors during office hours. Thousands of *Scouts* come there every year, to see the great number of exhibits of B.-P.'s decorations, of the presentations made to him by Scouts all over the world, and of historic letters, mementoes and trophies. It should not be missed by *Scouts* coming to London for a visit, singly or as a Troop or Pack.

The Restaurant on the top floor is open to members of the Movement for lunch and tea, from Monday to Friday, and its meals have attained a high reputation. Many Scouters drop in here during a visit to London. Parties of more than ten *Scouts* can be catered for, but only if at least four days' notice is given to the Manageress.

I have selected but a few of the Departments through which I.H.Q. does its best to fulfil its dual function of leading and serving the Movement. You will find the rest in "What I.H.Q. Does."

World Organisation

The organisation of international Scouting arose out of the first Jamboree at Olympia in 1920, and the first International Conference was held in Paris in 1922, when Great Britain became one of the founder-members of the world organisation. The world authority is the International Conference, to which each nation which has been admitted as a member is entitled to send six delegates. The Conference meets every two years, usually in connection with a World Jamboree or Rover Moot. Its purpose is to promote world unity of purpose and a common understanding in the fundamental principles of Scouting as laid down by the Founder; subject to that, it leaves each Scout nation free to run the Movement in its own country as it feels best.

An International Committee of 12 members is elected by the Conference and has power to act between meetings of the Conference, in accordance with a written Constitution. It appoints the Director of the International Bureau, who is the Committee's adviser and who runs the office, which is situated in London, but need not be.

Over the first 31 years of the Bureau's existence, it had only two Directors, and both of them were men of exceptional talents. The first was Mr. H. S. Martin, C.V.O., C.B.E., from 1922 to 1938, and the second Colonel J. S. Wilson, C.M.G., O.B.E. (formerly Camp Chief at Gilwell Park) from 1938 to 1953. On Colonel Wilson's retirement in 1953, the Committee appointed Major-General D. C. Spry, C.B.E., D.S.O., C.D., of Canada, as his successor.

At the time of writing, the latest published figures showed that there were 5½ million members of the Scout Movement in the world, coming from 54 countries. These are amazing figures and should be known to every Boy Scout. They vary from the enormous total of 3,183,266 in the United States of America to the miniature Movement in Liechtenstein, where the total population of 14,000 produces 269 *Scouts*—a higher proportion, it is believed, than anywhere else in the world.

But while figures are important, it is the spirit that matters most. In our common loyalty to the Founder and the principles which he laid down, the Scouts of the world have found a united spirit of friendliness and high purpose which is the envy of other international organisations. This spirit is difficult to describe, but easy to appreciate by anyone who attends a World Scout event. That is why every Group should strive to find a worthy representative at as many of these events as possible—not for himself alone, but for the Group as a whole.

CHAPTER 18

ODDS AND ENDS

THIS chapter contains notes on some miscellaneous points which did not fit in anywhere else. For convenience, they are set out in alphabetical order. Some of them are dealt with more fully in the I.H.Q. pamphlet " Business and Legal Notes," to which reference should be made wherever possible, as the law changes very rapidly in these days.

AWARDS

A number of awards have been instituted in the Scout Movement. They are the personal gift of the Chief Scout, and cannot be claimed as a matter of right. At the same time, he cannot possibly know of everybody whose work may have earned an award, and he welcomes submissions by District Commissioners and Local Associations, forwarded through County Commissioners.

Commissioners are asked to keep their eyes open for suitable cases, and G.S.M.s should let their D.C. know promptly of any case in which an award seems possible, particularly for gallantry or meritorious conduct.

If an award is made at Group level, it forms the occasion for a celebration, and suitable arrangements should be made for an impressive presentation. Good publicity can always be obtained in the local Press on such an occasion.

The awards are as follows: —

Cornwell Scout (P.O.R. 376-378)

Granted only to *Scouts* under 18 who have an outstanding record of service and efficiency, and have also shown great courage, endurance and gallantry. Cubs are eligible for this award. There has been a tendency to regard it as an award primarily for *Scouts* who have to endure a long period in hospital, possibly suffering from a mortal disease, but the Chief Scout is anxious that it should be by no means confined to such cases, deserving as they are. There is also a Certificate for cases which do not come up to the standard for the badge.

There is a fund at I.H.Q. from which grants may be made to holders of the badge who may need help in establishing themselves in a career.

Gallantry Awards (P.O.R. 380-384)

Available both to boys and adults for gallant acts involving some risk of life. Where there was no such risk, an award may nevertheless be given under the head of meritorious conduct (see below).

An award is sometimes given to a Group, or section of a Group, in respect of joint action.

A G.S.M. who hears of a gallant act in his Group which seems to him suitable for an award should take prompt action. It is necessary to obtain a full written account of the occurrence, backed by written evidence from eye-witnesses, wherever possible. These can best be obtained when the event is fresh in people's minds.

Good Service Awards (P.O.R. 390-392)

These are for adults only—either Scouters, or those who hold non-executive or honorary rank (P.O.R. 155-167). The District Commissioner and Local Association will be well aware of those who have rendered such outstanding service as to be eligible for an award, and action by G.S.M.s is not usually necessary. Scouters and others whose service has been long but not specially outstanding will be eligible for the Long Service Decoration (see below).

Long Service Decoration (P.O.R. 379)

In addition to the special awards for good services and meritorious conduct, a Long Service Decoration is given to a Scouter (and to certain non-executive ranks which are not at Group level) who has given 15 years' faithful and efficient service—in the case of a Scouter, as the holder of a warrant. The service need not have been consecutive, nor wholly in the same rank, but must have been wholly in one or more of the ranks specified in the rule.

Service as a *Scout* in any capacity cannot be counted.

It is the Chief Scout's wish that every Scouter who has given faithful and efficient service over this period should receive this decoration. A certificate by the District Commissioner and Local Association is necessary, but a G.S.M. should keep his Scouters' record of service before him, and should give the necessary information to the D.C. as soon as the 15 years' period has been completed.

Meritorious Conduct Awards (P.O.R. 385-389)

A number of cases arise where *Scouts* and Scouters display good qualities of courage, endurance, initiative or devotion to duty, but where a gallantry award is not available, because there has been no risk of life. For such cases, the Meritorious Conduct Awards have been instituted.

The Chief Scout sets a high standard for awards of this class, particularly for the Medal, and this should be borne in mind in considering whether an application should be submitted, but cases not reaching the standard for the Medal may be eligible for a Certificate or a Letter of Commendation.

Much the same evidence is required as is needed in the case of applications for Gallantry awards, and prompt action is called for.

In all cases falling within the above heads, early consultation with the District Commissioner is desirable. Appropriate forms for completion are provided by I.H.Q.

Two further expressions of appreciation may be mentioned here, but they are not awards in the above sense, and cases do not need to be submitted to I.H.Q. They are:

Thanks Badge (P.O.R. 371-375)

This was instituted by B.-P. in order that any *Scout* might express his appreciation of a good turn received from a member of the public. Nowadays, it is usually used as a means of expressing gratitude to a lay member, such as a member of a Group Committee or a farmer who provides a camp site. G.S.M.s will find that the badge is very highly valued by lay members who receive it, especially if it is not too lightly bestowed.

It is not intended for presentation to active *Scouts* or Scouters.

Permission must be obtained from the District Commissioner or Local Association, and the badge can be obtained from the Scout Shop on the order of the L.A. Badge Secretary.

Faithful Service Certificate

This is a nicely produced Certificate which can be bought at the Scout Shop, and is intended for use by a District Commissioner who wishes to make a presentation to a Scouter or lay member on retirement from Scouting or removal to another District. It is useful for cases which are not eligible for an award for good services or for the long service decoration. While the Certificate is presented by the D.C. and signed by him, there is no reason why a G.S.M. should not ask the D.C. to present it in a suitable case in the Group.

BADGES

Protection

All badges worn in the Movement are protected by law (P.O.R. 23) and may not be worn by anyone who is not a member of the Movement. We must therefore see that all reasonable steps are taken to protect them, and that they are not given away to outsiders as souvenirs. It is a good custom for the Group to issue badges free to *Scouts* who have qualified for them; the badges then remain the property of the Group, and can be claimed if a *Scout* leaves in discreditable circumstances. Normally, of course, the boy retains the badges as reminders of his days in Scouting.

Badges worn by Scouters

Scouters are expected to take the Scout Promise, and are then entitled to wear the Arrowhead badge worn by all members of the Movement, in cloth form attached to the uniform, or in metal when in ordinary clothes (P.O.R. 304 (i)).

This applies to Cub Scouters as to all others, but Cub Scouters who held warrants prior to 1st July, 1947, are permitted, if they wish to do so, to wear the Wolf's head badge. My own hope is that they will all wear the Arrowhead badge, for they have taken the Scout Promise, like other Scouters. It is sometimes argued that they should wear the same badge as their Cubs, but the simple answer to that argument is that anyone over 11 years old wears the Scout badge.

For those who prefer a rather less conspicuous badge in ordinary clothes, a small bronze Arrowhead is available (P.O.R. 305).

Some Scouters hold more than one rank in the Movement. They may not wear more than one of the badges at the same time. A Scouter who holds more than one warranted rank is expected to wear the badge appropriate to the duty he is carrying out at the time, but if this is not practicable, he wears the badge of the senior rank.

A Scouter who is also a Rover wears uniform as a Scouter on all occasions, for the warrant is the sign of the Chief Scout's confidence in him, but he may also wear on his uniform, if he so desires, the green shoulder-straps of a Rover (P.O.R. 306).

Scouters do not wear boys' proficiency badges, but a Scouter who is an interpreter may wear an emblem similar to that worn by Senior Scout interpreters, showing the language or languages spoken (P.O.R. 529).

Proficiency Badges

Examinations for proficiency badges are the responsibility of the Local Association, who appoint a panel of Badge Examiners.

It is very unfair to a boy who has worked hard for a badge that he should be kept waiting, either to be examined or to receive the badge when he has passed the tests. G.S.M.s should keep an eye on the Group arrangements in order to see that these things do not happen, and should take a case up with the L.A. Badge Secretary if the delay is due to the L.A. arrangements.

The object of the badge system is to encourage effort, not to reward brilliant attainment, and Badge Examiners are advised of this principle in the pamphlet "The Proficiency Badge Scheme." But a Badge Examiner will usually know nothing about a boy before he appears for his test, and will find it very helpful if the G.S.M. or section leader sends a note with the boy, giving him some information about the boy's general level of intelligence and attainment.

The section leader gives the boy a certificate in blank, which the boy gives to the Badge Examiner for signature if he passes. When a completed certificate is returned to the section leader, he should send it to the L.A. Badge Secretary at once, and the badge will be issued to him. Books of certificates can be obtained from Badge Secretaries. The Scout Shop supplies varieties of books for Wolf Cub, "under-15" and "over-15" badges, respectively.

COMPETITIONS

Nothing need be said about District or County competitions, except to repeat that the Group should enter for everything that is going on, whether or not it seems to have any chance of winning.

The G.S.M. will be wise to keep an eye on competitions within the Group, in order to ensure that over-keenness on the part of some of the boys does not lower Scout spirit.

We do well to avoid valuable trophies, and kind friends who feel inspired to present the Group with silver cups should be tactfully steered into spending their money in more useful ways. Boys are just as happy with things of little material value, such as a carved staff, a leather scroll, a miniature token, or even something quite ridiculous.

The Pack

At Cub age, boys are very prone to over-keenness, and competitions can mainly be reserved for Scouts. Certainly, any competition which continues over a period of a month or more is of little value. A Cub's effort is not sustained enough for that.

But inter-six games and other events can usefully be run on a competitive basis during a Pack meeting.

The Boy Scout Troop

Here the Patrol system is all-important, as indicated on pages 142-145, and competition will enter largely into

Troop meetings. Indeed, one Patrol may be encouraged to challenge another to a competition of their own devising at any time.

Troop competitions can be spread over a period of, say, three months. Some continue throughout the year, but many Scouters find that it is too long a period. A competition board hung up in the Headquarters and kept posted to date helps to maintain enthusiasm. The Court of Honour is entitled to be consulted as to what should be included in the competition. Inspections of persons and uniforms are always included, but attendance at Church parades should be outside its scope.

The Senior Scout Troop and the Rover Crew

Numbers are usually too small to enable much competition to take place within the Group. Where this is the case, inter-Troop or Crew challenges and District events can well be substituted.

DISPLAYS

I use this general term to include all Group shows to which the public is invited.

The I.H.Q. book, " Public Occasions," is full of good advice on all varieties of Group show. What follows is confined to some general advice to the G.S.M.

The motto is " the best possible on every occasion." We are putting ourselves on show, and a bad show is not only bad publicity, but also extremely discouraging to the boys.

Here are some potted notes on a variety of shows: —

Open or Parents' evening

A normal Pack or Troop evening, so that parents and friends can see what are the mysterious things their sons so obscurely refer to. No long speeches, but a few explanations, particularly of the higher mysteries such as Jungle Dances and the Grand Howl. A cup of tea, of course, and one or two parents versus sons games or competitions. The aim is to secure a family atmosphere. If the Assistant Scouters can run most of the programme, it enables the Cubmaster or Scoutmaster to get round and meet the parents.

Camp-fire evening

Best to keep the public out, unless you are lucky enough to have someone in the Group who can get the boys to sing and not shout, and who knows how to conduct.

Sale of work

So long as it is really Scout or Cub work that is being sold, and not stuff bought at the nearest store. But parents often like to have a stall or several stalls of their own, where more elaborate things can be sold.

Day at camp

This is extremely popular with parents, where the Troop is camping near home, say at Whitsun. The more ambitious Troops convey their parents by motor-coach (which has the incidental advantage that there can be a fixed time for all to depart). The Troop can run a camping type of programme, in order to show parents how they carry on in camp. The ladies will want to see cooking in progress.

The Group show

This is probably the public event of the year, and demands the most careful thought and preparation. Avoid the concert type of programme beloved of our ancestors, with recitations and piano solos alternating. A variety show is probably the best, as every member of the Group can take part, even if only behind the stage, and items can be rehearsed separately. There can be short concerted items by the Pack, and by each Patrol. But don't rule out the possibility of more serious plays, especially for the Seniors, and perhaps in co-operation with the Girl Guides or Rangers. In that event, you must have a really good producer.

It is essential that the show is well rehearsed, that there is a minimum of scenery to be changed, and that waits between items are avoided.

The custom of getting a V.I.P. to make a speech in the interval is in my opinion to be severely discouraged.

The business side of the Group show is quite considerable, and the framework of the arrangements needs careful planning by the G.S.M. There is the box office, which might be taken over by a member of the Group Committee, exemption from Entertainment Tax, licensing by the Lord Chamberlain if the Group is producing an original play or sketch, payment for copyright in respect of sketches used and of gramophone records played. For these things, reference to the pamphlet, " Business and Legal Notes," is strongly advised.

A good time for the Group show is during the Easter holidays, when small boys may be allowed to stay up later than in term-time.

EMBLEMS (P.O.R. 342-345)

An emblem, in the Scout meaning of the term, is a small patch of embroidered or printed material, not exceeding two inches in length or breadth, which is worn on Scout uniform if authorised by I.H.Q.

Some Counties have adopted an emblem for use by all members of the Movement in the County. Members of the Group will wear it in the position on the uniform (usually on the breast or shoulder) laid down by the County authorities.

Similarly, some Districts have obtained authority for the wearing of an emblem.

It may well be doubted, therefore, if a Group will find it desirable to ask for a separate emblem of its own. Too many badges become almost meaningless, and involve extra expense and more sewing for harassed mothers.

If, however, the Group decides that it would like to have such an emblem, the best place for it is on the point of the scarf. Careful attention must be paid to the directions of P.O.R., in order that approval may be obtained from I.H.Q., after the design has been submitted through the D.C. and County Commissioner. Approval will not be given for designs which exceed the prescribed size, or which are of a national character (*e.g.* the Scout or Cub badge) or contain the device of a national Saint, or the arms or crest of a family, or the title of the Group, or the name or initials of an individual.

FLAGS (P.O.R. 346-349)

Types sanctioned

(1) The National flag. The Union flag is used, but Sea Scout Groups may use the Red Ensign (in no circumstances the White Ensign).

(2) The Admiralty burgee, confined to Sea Scout Troops recognised by the Admiralty and issued to such Troops free of charge by I.H.Q.

(3) *Scout* flags. No special colour or design is insisted upon, but the advice of the Scout Shop may be sought, and a standard design including the Scout or Cub badge and the name of the Group, Troop or Pack is obtainable from that source. Some Groups have preferred a banner or burgee of heraldic type, but care must be taken to get skilled advice in order to avoid monstrosities.

Groups use their own discretion as to whether they have a Group flag and also one for each section, or only a selection of these.

As regards the Cub Pack, see also Totem Pole, pages 221-222.

(4) Patrol flags, carried on Scout staves by Patrol Leaders of Boy Scout and Senior Troops. A standard pattern, bearing the emblem of the Patrol animal or bird, is obtainable from the Scout Shop.

Use of flags

All flags should be treated with respect, but especially the National flag. Failure to respect the National flag is an act of discourtesy and distressing to the public. The I.H.Q. pamphlet, "Smartness in Scouting," deals with flag etiquette and with the correct way of carrying flags on parade.

As an act of respect, *Scouts* should salute National flags, when hoisted and broken, as well as uncased colours and *Scout* flags (but not Patrol flags). Experience shows that *Scouts* require instruction in these matters in their Groups, so that they may behave in the proper way when they are on their own.

The National flag is usually broken at the beginning of every *Scout* parade, and each morning in camp, the *Scouts* being called to the alert and saluting as the flag is broken. At the end of the parade, and at the close of the day in camp, the flag is lowered. It is a usual Scout custom to stand at the alert, but not to salute, at the lowering of the flag.

The *Scout* flag is used at the investiture of a *Scout*, being lowered to a horizontal position at the taking of the Promise, so that the Scouter in charge and the recruit may place their left hands on the flag.

It is necessary to be clear as to the procedure in connection with the lowering of flags on public occasions. National and *Scout* flags are lowered to the Queen, members of the Royal Family entitled to the prefix "Royal Highness," representatives of Her Majesty in Dominions and Colonies, foreign Monarchs and Presidents of Republics. They are not lowered during the playing of the National Anthem unless one of these persons is present. *Scout* flags only are lowered to the Chief Scout.

In Church, flags should be delivered and received by the flag-bearer and his two escorts, kneeling on the right knee.

The question is often raised as to whether *Scout* flags should be dedicated. It is strongly advised that this should not be done. It is the custom in this country that dedicated colours are not carried uncased except on parade, must not be moved without a colour party or escort, and must be carefully stored when not in use. This is difficult to obtain in the free and easy atmosphere of a Scout Troop, and moreover would normally prevent the flag being flown in camp. There is the further point that no one knows what should be done with a dedicated flag if the Group ceases to exist.

But if it is desired by a sponsored Group that a flag should be presented in Church, it can be done without dedication. A form of service which involves blessing the flag without dedicating it can be obtained from I.H.Q., and such a service can be used by open Groups in their own headquarters.

When it is necessary to drape the flags at a time of mourning (*e.g.* on the death of the Sovereign, or attendance at a funeral), approximately three yards of black material, four inches wide, should be tied in a bow with a nine-inch span above the flag, with ends hanging down for eighteen inches.

GIRLS

It is one of the difficulties of any organisation, devoted to boys only, to provide natural opportunities for the boys to meet girls in the course of the normal programme, but opportunities should be made as a necessary part of education for adult life. The wise leader will be able to create a healthy atmosphere and outlook.

Co-operation with the Girl Guide Movement has already been discussed in Chapter 15, and need not be pursued further. We must consider here the girls to whom our Scouts may become attracted, and they may or may not be Guides!

Cubs are no problem, nor are the younger members of Boy Scout Troops. They will not dodge a Pack or Troop meeting to go courting.

It is specially at Senior Scout and Rover stages that lads tend to be missing when wanted. Competition between the Scout programme and a date with a girl grows intense. It is no use getting annoyed about it. The Scouter must not only seek to make his programme as attractive as possible; he must also provide opportunities for the Scout to bring his girl along on suitable occasions. The boy must not feel that Scouting cuts him off from his girl, and that his going out with her is disapproved of by the Scouter. He will usually be sensible enough to reach an amicable compromise both with the Scouter and the girl, if the Troop is providing something worth while to come to.

In view of the small numbers in most Senior Scout Troops and Rover Crews, it may be hoped that District Commissioners will lend a hand by arranging some activities on a District basis where a lad can bring his girl along, but the main responsibility still lies with the Group.

Occasional social evenings, day rambles and hikes are in order, provided that they are not the only joint activity. Perhaps the girls may sometimes be the guests of the boys, and at other times may share the work by looking after the refreshments, while the boys lay the tables and wash up. When possible, they should share in devising the programme.

But on the whole it is better if boys and girls share some job of work, such as a joint good turn, or a debate, a discussion group or a dramatic show.

Church-sponsored Groups are often in the best position to deal with this problem through the Church's Youth Fellowship, to which both Senior Scouts, Rangers and non-Rangers belong. It is a good thing for Scouters to encourage their Seniors to join such Youth Fellowships and take as full a part in them as their time allows.

See also SEX EDUCATION (pages 218-220).

LIBRARIES

Some *Scouts* are voracious readers; some have not advanced beyond the comic strip. The good Group sees what it can do to persuade boys to cultivate the habit of reading and to improve their taste as they grow older. It makes it as easy as possible for boys to get hold of the best Scout books. Our best ally in these aims is the Public Library, ranging from the elaborate library in the large town to the travelling van in the village. I venture to assert that Scouters generally make insufficient use of the facilities which are available.

Everyone in the Group should be urged to join, however young. In many towns, Librarians provide special advice and attractions for youngsters in their children's libraries.

Special provision for *Scouts* and Scouters can usually be made by the Librarian, if he knows what is wanted. This is usually a matter to be negotiated at District level, but G.S.M.s might do a little quiet urging if nothing has been done. There are many instances where a Librarian has bought technical Scout books from a list supplied to him—books which are beyond the means of the individual or even the Group. Separate lists of books suitable for *Scouts* and Scouters are probably desirable. Much useful information for these lists can be gleaned from the book reviews in " The Scouter."

Some Librarians have even offered sets of books on loan to Scout Groups which have their own headquarters, and will change them from time to time. See what can be done in your neighbourhood.

The Local Association may have a small library of the more expensive Scout books, especially where there is a District headquarters where they can be housed. But whether or not there is such a library, there must be a Group library. It may be quite a simple box of essential books, kept in a cupboard where the Group equipment is kept. Where the Group has its own headquarters, it may be quite an elaborate affair, including boys' ordinary reading as well as Scout textbooks. Fine use can be made of such a library if you are lucky enough to secure the interest of a layman who is prepared to give time and trouble to understanding what boys like and to educating their taste.

The Scout Shop book list is useful in compiling a list of the essential books on Scouting. In this connection, it must be remembered that public libraries usually refuse to stock the cheaper and more flimsily-bound books, which get worn out very quickly.

POLITICS

The Scout Movement is strictly non-political (P.O.R. 13) and cannot take sides in a political issue. It follows that Scouters and other members of the Movement, when in uniform or acting as representatives of the Movement, must be equally careful not to enter into political issues, or to take part in political meetings.

We need to be particularly careful about this at a time when national and international events are arranged with a political end in view, although it may be disguised under such a harmless term as a "Peace Rally." The G.S.M. should get into touch with the District Commissioner before accepting an invitation to himself or his Group when he is in the slightest doubt about the wisdom of accepting it.

It follows similarly that the help of the Movement cannot be given to either side in the case of a strike or lock-out (P.O.R. 14). It may, however, happen that a strike or lock-out involves such grave public danger or inconvenience that a public authority calls for volunteers to keep essential services going. In such a case (fortunately very rare in this country), the rule is that the G.S.M. may, if the District Commissioner agrees, offer the help of the Troop, Senior Troop or Crew, provided that no compulsion is brought to bear on an individual to volunteer his services and that no penalty attaches to him for not volunteering.

But the fact that as a Movement we are non-political should not prevent the individual Senior Scout or Rover from studying political questions, whether local, national or international. Indeed, it is part of his training as a citizen that he should do so, in order that he may be able to use his vote intelligently when he is old enough. This may lead him to become a member of a political party, and as an individual he is perfectly free to do so, provided that he keeps the Scout Movement out of it. The same principle applies to Scouters, provided that they can wholeheartedly accept the Scout Promise and Law and that they make no attempt to preach party politics in uniform or to members of the Group. Especially at election times, it is good training for Senior Scouts and Rovers to discuss the important issues, being careful to see that all views are heard.

A word must be said here about Communism, for G.S.M.s must be sure that they and their Scouters understand the position. A pamphlet, "A Challenge to Scouting—the menace of Communism," has been specially issued, both by the Scout and Guide Movements, in order to explain where the Movement stands. This pamphlet should be in the possession of every G.S.M. It is enough to say here: —

(i) While under our democratic system the Communist party is free to put up candidates at elections and to preach its doctrines, it is obvious from what has happened in Russia and its satellite countries that when the Communists gain control they destroy existing parliamentary bodies and refuse to allow any party but their own. It is not therefore a good argument that we are indulging in party politics if we have nothing to do with the Communist party.

(ii) Wherever the Communists have gained control, they have suppressed the Scout and Guide Movements, because they are opposed to the ideals for which our Movement stands.

(iii) Communism denies the existence of a Divine Being, is opposed to the ideas of constitutional democracy which we accept when we promise to do our duty to the Queen, and does not follow the moral code laid down in the Scout Law. An active Communist Party member cannot in honour take the Scout Promise.

(iv) Our job in the Scout Group is to carry on our Scouting at the highest possible level, and to see that all our Scouters and *Scouts* are brought to realise progressively the full meaning of Scouting as an adventure of living under the guidance of God.

PUBLICATIONS

Appendix A contains a list of books and pamphlets which can be recommended to G.S.M.s as an aid to them in carrying out their own duties and in getting to understand the technical points involved in running the sections of the Group. The list necessarily excludes a great number of other books on Scout topics, and G.S.M.s are therefore recommended to obtain from the Scout Shop the current issue of their Book List, which includes not only books but also charts, pictures, posters, registers and records.

It is not expected that the Group will be able to afford to buy all these books, and reference should be made to the article on "Libraries" (pages 214-215).

SEX EDUCATION

Very careful thought has been given by I.H.Q. to the responsibility of Scouters in this connection, and a statement of policy was adopted by the Committee of the Council in September, 1948. This statement, with an introduction and a book list, has been published in a pamphlet entitled "Sex Education and the Scout Group." It is most important that all G.S.M.s should possess copies of this pamphlet and see that their Scouters know what it contains and carry out the policy laid down. A brief note such as this must not be regarded as a substitute for the pamphlet, but as a summary of it.

In the first place, the atmosphere of a vigorous and active Scout Group, securely founded on the Law and Promise, is itself of tremendous value to a boy as he grows into adolescence. Secondly, the boy's Scouter plays a very important part, even though he may never refer directly to the subject. As the statement of policy says: "The job of the Scouter is, first, to know his boys well enough to be able to realise when any of them want help; and, secondly, to ensure that they get the information and help they need. He can himself help the boy by showing in his own life and actions an example of one whose outlook to sex is clean and healthy, well-balanced, and securely founded in his own religion; by making the boy feel that in his Scouter he has an understanding and sympathetic friend; and, when occasion demands, by providing for the boy the best possible means to satisfy a legitimate desire for knowledge and to obtain help and advice in any time of difficulty."

The policy of the Movement in regard to direct sex instruction by Scouters is set out in the pamphlet in the following terms: —

"The Scouter must not regard himself as the person responsible for the giving of sex instruction to his boys, but rather as one of a team responsible for the boy's physical, moral and spiritual welfare; parents and other relations and adult friends, ministers of religion, and schoolmasters—all these should have their part in helping the boy to upright manhood. Generally, it is only when the Scouter finds that for some reason or other the boy is not getting the help he needs from the other members of this team that he should himself contemplate the giving of information.

"Where a Scouter feels that this duty is forced upon him personally, he must proceed with care and discretion. He must not himself undertake anything in the nature of formal instruction by means of lectures or classes. What instruction he gives must be done in an informal and friendly, but entirely matter-of-fact way, and in a manner suited to the individual boy or boys, using plain and simple words, and making sure he is understood. He should be careful to choose a suitable time and occasion, and to avoid any course that might be open to misconstruction. Generally, he ought not to give any instruction to a boy without first obtaining the acquiescence of the parents.

"Nevertheless, there may be exceptional occasions when a Scouter is faced with a situation that has to be dealt with there and then. The circumstances may be such that no delay could be contemplated and it would be out of the question to consult or inform anyone before taking action. In such a case, the Scouter must use his own judgment and do what he thinks best to help the boy or boys concerned.

"Finally, it must be remembered that the G.S.M. has a duty and a responsibility in this, as in all matters concerning the Group — namely, to help and advise his Scouters; and they on their side must consult him and get his advice and direction."

But, I repeat, this is no substitute for the pamphlet itself. In addition to the statement of policy as to direct instruction, quoted above, it contains much useful advice as to the differing treatment of this subject in the Pack, Troop, Senior Troop and Crew.

See also the article on "Girls" (pages 212-214).

SMOKING

The subject of smoking arises so often at Scout conferences that it may be worth saying a word about it here.

First, as regards Scouts. It is useless to adopt the attitude "Thou shalt not"; as B.-P. knew so well when he drafted the Scout Law, a negative command is a direct incentive to the human boy to do just the thing which is forbidden, but he will try to conceal it from authority.

Troop tradition through the Court of Honour is a great help, and if the Patrol Leaders set the right example, the younger ones will follow. They will say firmly that it is against the law of the land for a boy under 16 to smoke; therefore Scouts under 16 do not smoke in our Troop, for it is implicit in their Scout Promise that they obey the law. As regards Scouts over 16, we cannot stop them smoking if they insist on doing so. But we can encourage them to use their common sense, to realise what most of the best athletes and footballers do, in order to keep as fit as possible, and to calculate what they would be able to buy (such as the new rucksack they covet, or the trip abroad the Seniors are planning for next summer) if they did not spend the money on buying cigarettes.

I have sometimes heard Scouters say, "I never smoke in front of the boys." Frankly, this strikes me as humbug! If a Scouter feels like that about smoking, he should give it up altogether. And there is, of course, much to be said for a Scouter not smoking! But if a Scouter is a smoker, I can see no reason why he should not light his pipe or cigarette as he goes home after Troop parade or after a meal in camp.

A sense of fitness is our best guide. I am reminded of an experience of Lord Somers, who was startled to see a Scouter coming out of Church after a Church Parade strike a match on a tombstone, being the nearest spot available, and light up his cigarette in the churchyard.

But both Scouters and Scouts who smoke should make it a rigid rule that they never smoke at Group meetings or on other formal occasions. Perhaps you may think it so obvious a point that I need not have mentioned it. To which I can only reply that you may not have seen some of the Scouters I have seen on parade!

TOTEM POLE

Your Cub Pack probably has an object known as a Totem Pole, which may seem very odd to you if you are new to the game. But it is much treasured by the Cubs, and should not be regarded lightly. (A Pack can have a Club flag as well—see "Flags" (pages 210-211)—if desired.)

I have sometimes heard the Totem Pole described as "that heathen thing," but that betrays either ignorance or a completely wrong attitude of mind. If it were heathen, it would have no place at all in the Scout Movement. The Founder invented it as a symbol of the spirit of the Pack, with a Wolf's head at the top because it is the spirit of the Wolf Cub Pack that is being symbolised. It has nothing to do with totem worship.

If yours is a Church-sponsored Pack, or if your Pack is attending a District Church parade, there is no reason why the Totem Pole should not be proudly carried by the Pack, but it is usually placed at the back of the Church when you get there—not, I repeat, because it is a " heathen thing," but because the ordinary congregation or even the parson may not understand what it really signifies. But that is a matter for arrangement with the parson.

The design and use of the Totem Pole need not be discussed here, for the G.S.M. will probably not be allowed much say in the matter. Anyway, you will find it all in an I.H.Q. pamphlet, "Jungle Animals and Totem Poles."

CHAPTER 19

CONCLUSION

IN looking back at what I have written, I am conscious that most of it is concerned with business matters and a multitude of details, many of which may seem dull and uninspiring. I hope that the new G.S.M. will not feel that he has taken on a dull job. There will be dull moments, of course—what jobs are without them? There will be exasperating times, too, when other people seem to us silly because they won't take our advice. But the G.S.M. is mainly concerned with personal relationships — with Scouters, boys, parents and supporters—and these can be most friendly and rewarding, when inspired with the Scout spirit, which is so hard to define but so real in experience.

"This is all too much for one man to do in his spare time," someone may say. Of course it is. The "one-man band" is a menace to Scouting. The Group is run by a team, with the G.S.M., not as an overlord or dictator, but as the manipulator, the diplomat, the friend of all concerned, spreading the jobs around. It may well be said that the better the Group, the less the G.S.M. has to do.

But however businesslike we are, we must never become machine-like, for in all that we do it is the training and enjoyment of the boys that come first. We must approach our job in a humble spirit, for we are full of little failings ourselves, and the boys for whom we work are wonderful material. Let me quote from a speaker at a Scottish conference of many years ago: "Let us here pause and ask ourselves a straight, honest, searching question. 'How often do I really and truly remember that the young boys I work amongst are much better people than myself, who am supposed to be their leader and guide?' And yet how obvious a truth. In what do we surpass them? Age, stature, experience and its offspring, knowledge; mental concentration and will-power, perhaps. . . . I say we are shouldering *some* responsibility if we acknowledge, as acknowledge we surely must, that they are than ourselves not only physically more beautiful, but intellectually fresher, socially nicer, morally better."

If we appreciate our job in that human spirit, we shall get results, and, as the years go by, a deep spiritual satisfaction, as we see more and more boys growing up to be good men.

Let me conclude with two quotations, from men who have had years of service in Scouting and are able to look back upon failures and successes, upon moments of depression, fury and pride, and still say "It was well worth while."

The first quotation comes from a book by an American Scoutmaster named Rice E. Cochran, called "Be Prepared" (all of it worth reading if you can secure a copy): —

"Time has an alchemy all its own. It transmutes glum defeats into joyous victories with the passing of years. This is a reassuring knowledge to a Scoutmaster who goes forth to battle Mother Nature and stubborn flesh at some Scout encampment every month. My own twenty years with the Troop have been nerve-racking and scar-producing and sweaty; they have been sprinkled with rattlesnakes and angry mothers and flat tyres and sprained ankles and cold stew and whining boys and bellowing fathers and a million Troop meetings to plan and endless money to raise. I think I'll do twenty more."

The second quotation comes from Ted Neate: —

"You who are Group Scouters are in the first line—you have the grandest job of all, the direct training of the Cubs, Scouts and Rovers, the task which alone justifies the existence of the Movement. There is no greater trust in Scouting than that which is committed to you. But the Group is not yours, it is you who are the Group's. Neglect no means to increase your own capacity to carry out your job. Look wide and give your boys the same broad vision, and at the end of the day you will not be ashamed when they take their places in the world. Have you seen at a Group reunion the Rovers of to-day crowd round their old Akela? She's getting a little grey now, maybe, and the kids of ten years ago could pick her up and run round the clubroom with her, but she has the same smile for them. Have you seen the grand fellows back from the wars look the old man square in the eye and grasp his left hand again, and seen him fit to burst with pride? Have you known what it is to be honoured with the gratitude of your boys' fathers and mothers? Yes, you have seen these things, wherever you come from, and so have I, and I tell you there is no power and no influence in Scouting like the power and influence of the good Group."

APPENDIX A

LIST OF BOOKS, PAMPHLETS, ETC.

(A more complete list will be found in the Scout Shop Book List. Prices are so variable that they are not quoted in this Appendix.)

Books by the Founder, Lord Baden-Powell:

Scouting for Boys (*Pearson*)
Wolf Cub's Handbook, The (*Pearson*)
Rovering to Success (*Herbert Jenkins*)
Aids to Scoutmastership (*Herbert Jenkins*)

Other Books:

Baden-Powell (biography), Reynolds (*Oxford Univ. Press*)
Camping Abroad, Bincham (*B.S.A.*)
Duty to God in the Wolf Cub Pack, Mrs. Addis (*B.S.A.*)
God and the open Scout Group, Thurman (*B.S.A.*)
Handbook of Handicapped Scouting (*B.S.A.*)
How to run a Pack, Gilcraft (*Pearson*)
How to run a Troop, Gilcraft (*Pearson*)
Jungle Book, The, Kipling (*Macmillan*)
Jungle Book, The second, Kipling (*Macmillan*)
Pack Holidays and Cub Camping (*B.S.A.*)
Patrol Book Series (*B.S.A.*)
Patrol Leader's Handbook, The, Thurman (*B.S.A.*)
Prayers for use in the Brotherhood of Scouts (*B.S.A.*)
Public Occasions (*B.S.A.*)
Running a Troop, White & Bindloss (*Pearson*)

Scout Camps, Thurman & Hazlewood (*B.S.A.*)
Scouter Book Series (*B.S.A.*)
Scout Hymn Book, The (*B.S.A.*)
Scouting for Catholics and others, Reynolds
(*Burns, Oates*)
Scout Movement, The (history), Reynolds
(*Oxford Univ. Press*)
Scouts' Owns, Leonard (*Pearson*)
Scout Vocabularies, Andrew (*B.S.A.*)
Sea Scouting, Browne (*Pearson*)
Senior Scout Handbook, The (*B.S.A.*)
Standing Camps, Morgan (*B.S.A.*)
Wolf Cubs, Gilcraft (*Pearson*)

Booklets and Pamphlets (published by B.S.A.):

Air Scouting
Alternative Tests (for Handicapped *Scouts*)
Bibliography (book list for Scouters)
B.-P. Guild of Old Scouts (published by B.-P. Guild)
Business and Legal Notes for Scouters
Camping Standards
Challenge to Scouting, A
—the menace of Communism
Cubbing—a word to parents
Deep-Sea Rover Scouts
Group Committee, The
How to start a Pack
How to start a Troop
Integration of Scout and Guide units into
the life of the Church
Jungle Animals and Totem Poles
Local Associations
Notes for Women Scouters
Our own place
"Over-15" (the Senior Scout scheme of training)
Policy, Organisation and Rules
Proficiency Badge Scheme, The

Religious Obligations of Scouts, The
Rover Plan, The
Scouting—a word to parents
Scouting for the Handicapped Boy
Scouting in Preparatory Schools
Scouting in Secondary Schools
Scouting, Religion and the Churches
Sea Scouting
Sex Education and the Scout Group
Smartness in Scouting
Sponsored Group, The
This is addressed to you (briefing for National Service)
Training of Scouters, The
Use and Recruitment of Manpower, The
What I.H.Q. Does
What is Scouting?

Leaflets (published by B.S.A.):

Exemption from Control of Camping
Insurance, Policies—leaflets
Use of Lorries by Scouts, The

Periodicals:

The Scouter, monthly
The Scout, weekly
Jamboree, monthly

INDEX